CROSSCURRENTS *Modern Critiques*
Harry T. Moore, *General Editor*

CROSSCURRENTS *Modern Critiques*

David Holbrook

Dylan Thomas
AND POETIC DISSOCIATION

WITH A PREFACE BY

Harry T. Moore

Carbondale

SOUTHERN ILLINOIS UNIVERSITY PRESS

For Wilfrid Mellers

DYLAN THOMAS cast a spell with the bright and dark richness of his writing, and with the bardic ecstasy he gave to the reading of his poems before audiences and at recording sessions. In the present book, David Holbrook resists the charms of Thomas and presents a minority report on him which deserves hearing. Note that I say Thomas rather than Dylan, though when I knew him I called him Dylan, as everyone else always did—Mr. Holbrook thinks this was one of the signs of the poet's perpetual immaturity; and just now there is a successful play called Dylan!

Mr. Holbrook admits Thomas's gifts but doesn't find in him the satisfaction he finds in some of the authors of the past, such as Chaucer and Keats. But this doesn't mean that Mr. Holbrook is a hidebound traditionalist: although he rejects some of T. S. Eliot's later poetry, he accepts The Waste Land and James Joyce's Ulysses, and these works are, even at the present moment of antiliterature and the literature of the absurd, still in the avant garde. Mr. Holbrook explains very readily and in detail what he finds disturbing in Dylan Thomas: a metaphoric irresponsibility, a lack of maturity, a tendency toward self-destruction, and other matters I will let Mr. Holbrook enumerate and explain for himself.

His book is a shock, a challenge, but it is also an important revaluation, not only of Dylan Thomas, but of much else in poetry written in English. Mr. Holbrook's arguments begin just beyond this page, and you may follow them for yourself. Whatever your measure of agreement or otherwise, your attention will be magnetized.

HARRY T. MOORE

Southern Illinois University
July 31, 1964

ACKNOWLEDGMENTS

THE AUTHOR is grateful to David Higham Associates, Messrs. Dent, and the Executors of the late Dylan Thomas for permission to reproduce *There Was a Saviour, Was There a Time,* and other extensive quotations from that writer's work. The author is also much indebted to those who have helped him produce this book in the course of many rewritings. He is grateful to his students in adult classes. He thanks Mr. Michael Black of Cambridge University Press for reading the manuscript and making many valuable suggestions, and Mr. Geoffrey Grigson for meticulous comments which saved the author from several excesses. Mr. Harold Mason has earned his gratitude—and one hopes the reader's—by urging the elimination of uncertain and wrong-toned matter. The author's wife deserves more than the conventional tribute for reading and rereading this book beyond the limits of endurance, and, while having at times doubt about the author's motives, never discouraging him from a task of uncertain outcome.

Some revisions have been made in this edition for publication in the United States, particularly in the Introduction.

DAVID HOLBROOK

CONTENTS

Dylan Thomas
AND POETIC DISSOCIATION

1 INTRODUCTION

THOSE QUALITIES I find most satisfying in poetry of the past I seldom find in contemporary poetry. In current reviewing one seldom finds the work of any poet writing before 1900 used as a touchstone; there has been assumed, as it were, a complete break in continuity, so that twentieth-century poetry stands—or is taken to stand—as a new *genre* in its own right.

Yet there is plenty of poetry "about"—published, seriously discussed. But what seems to me to thrive in this situation is a kind of poetry which is a reproduction of the genuine article. It goes through the motions of the real thing: but it is fundamentally deficient in texture, rhythm, movement—in life, indeed. Perhaps this is much to be explained by the loss of vitality of common speech and because our common language has lost the habit of seeking to understand life through metaphor. Our language no longer seeks, as folk idiom sought, moral truths and attitudes to life as a natural habit. There are other reasons, to do with a lowering of expectations of what art can and should *do* for us. For me the effect is that most modern poetry, since, say, T. S. Eliot's *Four Quartets*, yields few satisfactions of the kind I get from Keats or Chaucer.

These feelings of dissatisfaction have been the spur to writing this book, in order to attempt to explain to myself why they centered round the work of Dylan Thomas. I felt that only by a rejection of Thomas's poetry, his attitude to poetry, and the attitudes of his audience to poetry could this essential activity of the civilized consciousness, poetry, regain health and effectiveness. This negative task—I hope it has a positive effect—has not been an easy one. So much suggests itself for discussion that seems to have little to do with poetry. But in order to seek to reject the spurious and to touch the vital I have struggled to confine myself to poetry—to actual poems and lines of verse, so that we may sharpen our hearing. If we can do this, I think we may even then hear a poignant true voice in some of Dylan Thomas's poems—drowned as it is by the false voice which he invented to hide from us and from himself the nature of his incapacities.

But I recognize now that this book is at one with the weakness I seek to point out—inevitably infected by the dissociation Dylan Thomas seems at times deliberately to have brought down on his own head. The reader must therefore not expect my tone to be perfect or the structure of the book to be clear and orderly. All I can hope for is that the sequence of discussions moves towards something of a conclusion—that poetry—if it is alive, and not manufactured opportunistically to concoct a reproduction of the genuine article—cannot be but metaphorically responsible.

What I mean by "metaphorically responsible" I hope will be made clear as I examine that poetry which seems to me to have a "true value." It is not easy to indicate in a book exactly what the true voice of poetry sounds like, because one needs to be able to read lines aloud, so that subtleties of rhythm—how the poetry "goes"—may be indicated. It is in these that one can detect genuineness, as in "No worse, there is none. Pitched past pitch of grief . . ." or "No, Time, thou

shalt not boast that I do change . . ." or "I wonder, by
my troth, what thou and I / Did, till we loved?" In
such lines one can hear the voice of a man speaking
with the rhythms and inflections of conviction, with an
assurance which convinces one that the writer cares
about what he is saying. To distinguish between such
poetry, and the verse of Dylan Thomas, as spoken by
him, would not be at all easy—since it is also obvious
that Thomas believes in what he is saying, too, in a way.
It would be a delicate matter to examine those inflections and rhythmic patterns, by which one would want
to indicate that Thomas's impulse is to believe in that
which protects him against truth, while those of Hopkins, Shakespeare and Donne are to come closer to
it.

Yet that is what I hope to try to do, by analysing
Thomas's poetry in this book. In doing so I shall be
seeking to distinguish between that poetry which is
impelled to try to build bridges between inner and
outer reality, and that which erects barriers, and fosters
dissociation. I think there is a kind of imaginative
activity that may be called "life-promoting," because it
accepts the responsibility of moving back and forth
between the unknown areas of our experience and the
known—as metaphor does. I think there is another
kind which may be associated with certain impulses to
hallucinate, rather than to explore experience by vision.
There is a kind of employment of the powers of
phantasy which seeks to project a false picture over the
face of reality, to disguise its nature from ourselves—a
kind of closed circuit vision, really narcissistic. It does
what drugs or alcohol do—separates us from a reality
which has become too painful. This differs essentially
from the vision which bravely persists in exploring the
nature of man, and the nature of the external world, to
gain insight, understanding and effectiveness. The lat-

ter inevitably requires adjustment of the whole personality and the acceptance of the tragic conditions of
human existence. It means the forfeiting of certain
beliefs dear to our nostalgic impulses—for the closer
we come to the reality of ourselves and the world, the
more we are forced to relinquish vestigial beliefs in
omnipotence, magic, or idealised perfection, in ourselves and others. We are also forced to come to terms
with the bad in ourselves and others. This is the true
tragic process.

The origins of these diverse uses of phantasy—the
false and the true—are in our infant experience. Inevitably, we give only a crude account of these in our
terminology of perception and cognition, because the
stages of the origins of consciousness belong to states of
mind in which "knowing" and "perceiving" are rudi-
mentary. But roughly we may say that many of our
adult difficulties stem from faults which develop at
those stages of the formation of consciousness when
the infant's phantasy and its feelings are strong, but its
sense of reality is unformed—even to the extent of its
not knowing the difference between "me" and "not-
me." For instance, when the baby is hungry, as Freud
suggested, it hallucinates—tries to "make" a feeding
mother who shall "satisfy" it by illusion. It finds that
this fails, but in the course of it the baby has formed
the image of a "perfect" and "controllable" mother
who will give him everything he wants. When the
mother does arrive, she "fills in" the vision, by, as it
were, meeting him half-way, helping him to complete
the true image of herself, at a time when he does not
yet know "what it is he has to hallucinate." [1]

Later, the child experiences other difficulties in
coming to terms with reality. For instance, while he
believes that he can "make" the mother, by hallucinat-
ing her just as she is about to appear, he also begins to

feel concern about the real effects of his angrier and more destructive phantasies in which he seeks to destroy or consume the mother. Bad feelings (such as rage and hunger in himself) he also tends to project over the mother, who seems to him therefore to persecute and threaten him. One of his chief problems is to come to terms with this "bad" mother—and later with the "bad" in himself, as his sense develops, of what is "me" and "in me," and what is out there, in the "not-me."

This stage coincides with the period at which the child also becomes aware of the mother's separate existence—and develops fears that the mother, from whom he takes in all goodness, may go away and leave him—whereupon he would cease to exist. But all these tremendous stages in psychic growth, painful as they are, are also necessary stages in the development of our powers of consciousness and perception. Without them there would be no consciousness. But the crises leave inevitable flaws, because no one can pass through these enormous crises of inward life without suffering damage—because our environment is always not quite good enough. One of the crucial problems is that of separation—when the mother removes herself, the child seeks by all kinds of hallucinations to "make" her, to exert a sense of power to "control" her, and so on. By leaving the child for periods, the mother throws him back on his own resources, and gradually he has to come to terms with reality—accepting her separate existence, relinquishing omnipotence, and allowing that he must abandon his vision of the "perfect" mother, and the nostalgically recalled "total bliss" of intrauterine and immediate post-natal life, for ever. The baby really experiences at this stage, usually at weaning, the sense of being forever cast out of Eden— into a world in which "in the sweat of thy face shalt thou eat bread." His psychic woes are the curse of Adam. And they lead him ever after, as an adult, to seek for a perfection that is never possible on earth, to seek a perfect "lost" mother who can never be found, and to try to believe in hallucinations, which are projected over the face of reality, rather than in reality itself. But they also impel him to seek "the good" by reparative impulses. Because these developmental processes in the growth of such a fine and delicate instrument as human consciousness can never go completely "right," we are all flawed—all suffer the curse of Adam. And so, everyone has a "reality problem"—a problem of needing to gain more and more insight into their own make-up, weaknesses, distorted motives—and to gain understanding of the outside world, and consequent effectiveness in dealing with it, by creative and reparative activity. Insofar as we fail to deal adequately with the outside world, and with ourselves, we are still held back by inadequate development of our reality sense— of stages which have never been completed in infancy.

Art is a means of building bridges between inner and outer reality, and of thereby helping us develop our reality sense, gain insight, form a sense of our own identity; of helping us to understand human nature in general and to come to terms with human experience, seen in its larger context. It helps us to build up a sense of significance and hope, by constructive experience. In this activity, as in the infant's psychic development, phantasy is crucial, and metaphor is the means by which illumination is gained, since much of our inner reality can only be expressed and understood in metaphorical terms, as in dreams. The poetic apprehension enables us to apprehend inner reality, as science helps us to apprehend outer reality. One reality is certainly no more "real" than the other—they are complementary.

In art criticism, then, our problem is to discriminate between those expressions of experience which help to build bridges, and those which, like the infant's attempts to deceive itself by hallucination, stave off certain necessary recognitions of the truth. Because the truth of our mortal existence is painful, inevitably we display through life the same tendency as the infant has to resist the acceptance of reality. In this lies the roots of dissociated phantasy—that which exerts a strong energy in the direction of avoiding reality and defending the self against it.[2]

Dylan Thomas's poetry I consider poetry of this dissociated phantasy. For reasons which I will try to explore, he found adult reality impossible to tolerate and accept. The only way to integrated consciousness in the infant is through the gradual pains of disillusionment, at the hands of a mother who can enable the child to bear this by her continuing and loving presence. Without crises and pains, there is no viableness and no consciousness—the result is inanition, dissociation as in mental illness, or death. Similarly, in the adult, a severe dissociation from reality will be fatal—the inability to deal with life will eventually cause total breakdown.

This was so in Dylan Thomas's case. Culturally the problem now becomes one which may be stated thus: how is it that such a flight from life, toward dissociation which could only prove fatal to adult powers, can become the object of such a cult, and so acceptable to a popular audience? What light does this cast on the nature of our literary culture now?

There is, of course, a fashion in recoil from life, and this is a mark of schizoid culture which finds it hard to tolerate deep, committed feeling—what Ian D. Suttie[3] called the "taboo on tenderness." We may inherit this disability from parents who fear giving in love, who are unable to afford the disturbing flux of feelings in affection. Those who grew up from a childhood in which the flux of love has been so inhibited may suffer grave inadequacies in their mature powers, not only in loving but also in maintaining a grasp on personal and external reality. Love has not grown in them, and they recoil from its exigencies on the whole being. This kind of dissociation, caused by failures in nurture, would seem to have become exacerbated since the industrial revolution (there is plenty of uninhibited tenderness in folksong), possibly by the breakdown of traditional forms of community and family life, and possibly by the mechanization of the human soul, the degradation enforced on men by monotonous and exhausting tasks in ugly and oppressive surroundings: D. H. Lawrence protests bitterly against this reduction of the tender and vital powers in a man by industrial life, because he witnessed it in his father.[4]

In literature detached from popular roots the dissociation from the reality of life and of feeling has often become associated with a yearning for a romantic nonphysical existence, for the *"altitudes de la métaphysique de l'Amour, aux glaciers miroirs que nulle haleine de jeune fille ne saurait tenir de buée pour y tracer du doigt son nom avec la date!"* This easily becomes associated with the cult of remote aestheticism, and with its obverse in the impulse to shock—that desire to exhibit life's grosser elements sensationally, in a depressive way, whose falsity lies in the implicit denial of the reality of good. Such notes as these have these impulses in common:

> *Foetus mal conservés saisissant d'une lieue*
> *L'odorat et collant leur faces jaunes et bleues*
> *Contre le verre du bocal!* [5]
>
> GAUTIER.

> *With the thirst and the hunger of lust though*
> *her beautiful lips be so bitter,*
> *With the cold foul foam of the snakes they*
> *soften and redden and smile.*
>
> SWINBURNE.

> *Cupid, astride a phallus with two wings,*
> *Swinging a cat-o'-nine tails.*
>
> POUND.

> *Je ne vis plus*
> *Qu'une outre aux flancs gluants, toute pleine*
> *de pus!*
>
> BAUDELAIRE.

> *Along the garden wall the bees*
> *With hairy bellies pass between*
> *The staminate and pistillate,*
> *Blest Office of the epicene . . .*
>
> ELIOT.

We have a great deal of this kind of cultivated recoil from life in modern poetry, and it has been one good reason for indifference in many readers. But common natural protest against lapses of taste has become disarmed by acclaim and inept criticism, and in Dylan Thomas we find a force built into his phantasy and the projection of himself that has an extraordinary power to disarm criticism. Take for instance these lines of Dylan Thomas's, the subject of calm discussion by Mr. John Bayley in *The Romantic Survival*, and by Miss Edith Sitwell:

> *And, from his fork, a dog among the fairies,*
> *The Atlas-eater with a jaw for news,*
> *Bit out the mandrake with tomorrow's scream.*

Thomas's gloss on these lines is, "a world-devouring ghost creature bit out the horror of tomorrow from a gentleman's loins." Edith Sitwell (not literally enough for the poet) had said of the lines "They refer to the violent speed and sensation-loving, horror-loving craze of modern life." In fact the interpretation is really anyone's guess, but we may take it that the lines refer to humanity (whose mandrake, when uprooted tomorrow, will scream, whatever thay may mean) which is having, in these lines, its genitals bitten off by a dog-like creature. (At this point the reader may ask himself whether the "horror-loving" epithet of Miss Sitwell's may be applied to "modern life" or certain gestures in poetry?)

Quite coolly, however, mentioning in his course Yeats, Arthur Symons, Maeterlinck and Shelley, Mr. Bayley discusses Thomas's lines, their castration image, and brings himself to say, "*Search* for Thomas's meaning is a dangerous process." Indeed it is, as one finds when he next quotes Thomas's own continued gloss on the lines quoted above:

> The mouth of the creature (the Atlas-eater) can taste already the horror that is not yet come, or can sense its coming, can thrust its tongue into news that has not yet been made, can savour the enormity of the progeny before the seed stirs, can realize the crumbling of dead flesh before the opening of the womb that delivers the flesh to tomorrow.

Mr. Bayley goes on to comment, "The lines show Thomas's obsessional theme, the telescoping of existence." The coolness reveals a difficulty one has when dealing with Dylan Thomas: the critics refuse to discuss the words, and, under the poet's "verbal banter," refuse, too, to see the handling of language as a creative activity with any bearing on life.

Thomas's words, in his gloss, have as their preponderant image that of a genital kiss, first on the "mandrake" which once bitten away gives place to the "womb" (which in Thomas is often a "wound"), and then becomes the "crumbling of dead flesh." How can such imagery be so coolly discussed without blindness to language and life? It is not that the lines and the gloss are disgusting [6] (though they are that), but that, having their roots in oral sadism, they disperse a recoil from life, by a damaging sensational necrophilia. It is not that we have here a poetry which, in its "indifference to moral ideas" (to use Matthew Arnold's words) is a poetry of "indifference to life"—but a poetry whose effect is to vindicate negative impulses—the flight from life or the denial of it—by involving us in disarmed acceptance of a morbid obsession with "bad" elements of reality, at the expense of the whole and wholesome.

These manifestations of sensational morbidity in present day poetry have a compulsive energy—the poets are often seeking to draw us into becoming involved in attitudes which make special pleas for the poet's own derangements and imbalances. The effect of this energy on us is disturbing—but disturbing in unsatisfying ways. We are offered no deeper self-knowledge, no advanced understanding of reality or ourselves through metaphor. We are only bewildered and aroused into a confused excitement—as we are, say, by a horror film. Too often the poet seeks not to involve us in sympathy, but to shock us into sharing his self-protective inhibitions—of his sympathy and feeling—and into joining him in his dissociation from reality. (Henry Miller does the same in prose).

In seeking to involve us thus in dissociated attitudes to reality, the poet may contribute to the weakening of our powers of dealing with reality. This activity of phantasy is thus at the opposite pole to that of art which is truly "life-promoting." There is, however, the additional problem that some "neurotic" poetry, or even the outpourings of schizophrenics, can, by giving us insight into aspects of existential experience, illuminate our understanding of human nature.[7] It is possible that some of Dylan Thomas's poetry may do this for us. But first we must learn to resist those blandishments by which he is driven, for his own purposes, to convince us of the truth of a distorted vision, trying to make us accept a partial as a whole picture.

The connection between Thomas's dissociated poetry and his life, though I do not want to discuss biographical details, is obvious if we turn to a psychoanalytical statement of the typical manifestations of the self-destructive alcoholic. Karl Menninger's classical psychoanalytical account [8] not only fits Thomas as a personality—it also gives us clues as to the nature of his strange disarming appeal, and the unconscious modes by which he maintained it:

> It is true that alcohol has the quality of giving some degree of relief from the pain of facing reality and also from other psychic pain resulting from emotional conflicts . . . the use of alcohol can be regarded as an attempt at self-cure. . . . [We might well substitute here the word "poetry" for alcohol.] Some alcoholics recognise this but many others cannot be persuaded that their periodic bouts are more than jolly little affairs which, for all they may end in a rather untidy and tiresome mess, with a few disappointments all round, no one should hold against them. The wish to be treated like a child and to have one's most serious aggressions overlooked is very characteristic of the type of personality which finds excessive indulgence in alcohol so irresistible. . . . Such individuals, as children, have endured bitter disappointment, *unforgettable* disappointment, *unforgiveable* disappointment! They feel, with justification, that they have been betrayed, and their entire subsequent life is a prolonged, disguised reaction to this feeling.
>
> It is true that every child meets with disappointment and frustration; this is inevitable in the nature of reality

. . . We all had to be weaned, we all had to relinquish our belief in Santa Claus. In this respect, then, the
alcoholic probably does not suffer in childhood anything qualitatively different from what the rest of us
suffer, but apparently there is a quantitative difference.
In the case of the alcoholic the disappointment has
actually been greater than he could bear. It was so
great that it definitely affected his personality development so that in certain respects he remains all his life
what we call an 'oral' character . . . one characterised
by conspicuous residua of the stage of psychological
development in which the child's attitudes toward the
world was determined by his wish to take it in through
the mouth and to destroy with his mouth anything
which resisted his demands.

In drinking the alcoholic performs with his mouth,
takes in a magical substance, and may become aggressive. The same elements are found in the oral imagery
and babble-quality of Dylan Thomas's poetry, its magical attitude (as of incantation) to reality, and what
John Bayley calls "the sense of being assaulted by
something other than words." The poetry, like the
drinking, belongs to oral sadism, to an infantile revenge
reaction—and this is quite clearly expressed in some
poems, as in phrases such as "I make this in a warring
absence."

The other connection that needs to be made here is
between Thomas's recoil from sexual reality, and his
own frenetic sexual activity in life. Menninger speaks
of the "typical sexual pattern in alcoholism relating the
aggressive and guilt-feelings to the erotic value of the
drinking," and says,

It is almost axiomatic that alcoholics, in spite of a great
show of heterosexual activity, have secretly a great fear
of women and of heterosexuality in general, apparently
regarding it as fraught with much danger. They often

realize that they do not possess normal sexual powers or interests, frankly avowing that it is not sexual gratification they seek from women so much as affection, care, love—by which they mean maternal solicitude.

We shall see these elements in Thomas's poetry.

In Dylan Thomas's life and in his poetry we witness the poignant quest of an adult to find the (mother) love he remains unconvinced of having had as a child. To be convinced of being loved for ourselves is the way to full adult living: without the conviction maturity is feared and denied. So, Thomas's deep fear of mature reality is a complement to his promiscuity, as is symbolized by his recurrent images of sexual potency being dissolved in alcohol or some other form of oblivion. (Kingsley Amis manifests the same symptoms, and they are the basis of his destructive comic appeal.) These suggest not only an inability to find the reality of love, but a total failure of the reality sense, as in the poetry (which is why Thomas matters to literary criticism). Rather than being apocalyptically larger than life, Dylan Thomas's vision is essentially still in the condition of the infant's "false" hallucination—and so can offer us far less, in terms of bridges between inner and outer reality, than the cult of this "baby-man" would lead us to suppose. His popularity and his wide sales are less an index of a revival of poetry than an indication that the poetic sensibility, in poet and reader, has become yet more dissociated in our time and that poetry itself reflects the general schizoid tendencies of our culture.

2 THE TRUE VOICE
OF ENGLISH POETRY

WHAT ARE the linguistic exigencies of metaphorical responsibility? Poetry operates by all the qualities of language. These qualities cannot be manipulated into life, they can only come to life, from the strange psychic sources of order deep in our whole beings, as we seek to make sense of our experience by moving in creative explorations between inner and outer reality. The combination of all these qualities is in the natural life of ordinary language: they *are* language. But though we all have the power naturally as children, only an adult intensely responsive to language in all its organic life in every manifestation can use language as an artist. And by responsive I do not simply mean that the hair stands up on the back of his neck when he hears Keats read aloud, or that he can produce exegesis which is acutely satisfying intellectually. The responsiveness to language which the writing and reading of literature demand is that which knows language to be a means to living in a civilized way rather than merely existing as sentient brutes. The forms of our emotional life, our impulses towards others, our perception of the material world, our ability for ordered thought and feeling, our civilization and spiritual life depend primarily upon forms of language. If the subtlety and variety of our sense of rhythm, pattern, texture in language decline, so does our ability to live; which is why those who are concerned with language know the misuse of language in mass communications to be a dangerous threat not merely to "democracy" but to the whole vitality of the life of the community; not because "misuse" weakens "people's ability to think for themselves," but because it destroys the habit of exploring the nature of life by the rhythm and texture of language with its full emotional body—as the rural dweller in his idiom used to explore them. To weaken language weakens our very hold on life.

A clergyman philologist of the early nineteenth century wrote that "The real and natural life of language is in its dialects" (R. Forby, *The Vocabulary of East Anglia*, 1830): the destruction of local dialects during the last century in England, however necessary for a standardized industrial society, has weakened the life of our language as a whole, and what has been lost from the language has been largely its poetic habits. Educated poetry has been insufficiently enriched in the same period by contact with popular life.

In poetry the use of language should be at its finest. This is T. S. Eliot's self-conscious preoccupation in his *Four Quartets*. What are the qualities of language which poetry must refine and invigorate? Is it that poetry must function as the scientist would find it convenient for language to function, reducing language to a precise tool by excluding its aura of uncertainty and emotional ambiguity? To make the word a symbol, like x?

Something quite different, poetical statement achieves its definition by bringing together the complexities of emotional ambiguity to enact a meaning, so that we can possess, with some effort and to some degree, the exact experience which the poem embodies. It is a poetical experience, which is not to be confused with an actual experience; we enjoy grief in poetry, but we do not enjoy grief in reality. Ordinary life can be ugly, disordered; poetry always offers not only order in the experience, but by the pattern of the poem and its "inscape," offers us a degree of attitude to the experience. And these things take place at the intuitive level, where the enhanced insight and understanding can actually change personality. That is, we are left as after being trained to play an instrument or dance, with new potentialities in our minds, muscles, nerves, our whole make-up: but of course to deal with more complex modes of living than mere ability to perform. We are armed with more adequate and felt patterns of interpretation: our appetences—such as govern our preparedness to face new experiences—are conditioned by concepts of significance. The unpredictable processes of time and coincidence incessantly assail us: but by imaginative exploration beforehand we are prepared to deal with fresh aspects of reality. We possess the wisdom of our race, through words, and can live a little better by it. We can draw on the experience of the dead, for living purposes.

Let me take some lines of poetry to examine the qualities of poetry. It is impossible to produce a catalogue of poetry's "ingredients"—because at no time are the ingredients separable; we only schematize them after the event, as grammarians do rules of grammar, by conscious intellectual effort. The satisfaction we derive from this schematizing and analysis may be confused with the real response to the poetry, and this is what has happened to some of our critics, particularly since William Empson's example of profuse ingenuity (his own early work being often exact by the fineness of his sensibility rather than by his analytical intellectual powers—many imitators, alas, had insufficient sensibility). But it is possible and valuable to discuss what appear to be separate elements of poetic communication, so long as one keeps specific pieces of poetry in front of one.

The first task is perhaps to show how ancient a tradition each English word may have. When a poet writes he takes on, in relation to our living now, the burden of responsibility to what we inherit from six hundred years' growth of the English language. To demonstrate this I shall take a line from *Sir Gawaine and the Grene Knight*, because this poem springs fully clad from the original creative moment of our English civilization, its language, and it consciousness. So much so, and so much does it convey the underlying vigour of the rural idiom of mediaeval English life, inseparable from that community's attitudes to life, that it speaks of a relish and vitality in English life which in certain areas of our make-up we seem to have lost gradually over the six centuries since, but which we can recapture by reading this poem.

The line I wish to discuss, to begin to explore the nature of metaphor and the qualities of language, is this: "The snawë snitered ful snart, that snayped the wyldë." Now in the Early English Text Society edition of *Sir Gawaine*, the hanging footnote says "Snow falls," which is virtually what the poetic *statement* can be said to be. There is a clause added to say that the snow "snayped" the wild life, but the main statement is, Snow falls. Now anyone with a preconceived idea, say, that poetry consisted of a series of *images* would be lost with our line, for it has nothing of the sharp clarity of image of Shakespeare's "And birds sit brooding in the snow," or Edward Thomas's "Over the land freckled with snow half-thawed . . ." Nor would the person who believed *onomatopoeia* to be the essence of poetry (or the "mere sound") be as confident here as he would be with the next line: "The werbelandë

wyndë wrapped from the hyghë," where the "werbelandë" sound gives the soughing of wind in the trees
and "wrapped" the flapping of coat, or shutter, or
banging of boughs in the wind rush. Snow falling
makes no sound and "snitered" and "snart" evoke no
appropriate sound like Hardy's "And there is no waft
of wind with the fleecy fall," except perhaps by the
choice of the alliterative "s." To see what kind of
quality of language we have in the line we may be
helped if we examine "the natural life of language
. . . in its dialects." The Reverend R. Forby, already
mentioned, writing in 1830 of East Anglian dialect,
comes to discuss the habit in vernacular Norfolk of
corrupting "literary" words into expressive rural ones—
such as "solintary," "screwmatic"—and this brings him
to the discussion of "archaic" words in dialect: what he
really has discovered is that dialects preserved expressive words which occurred in early English literature,
but which had disappeared from educated literature as
the educated classes gradually lost touch with popular
culture after the seventeenth century. And, while losing
touch, educated language purged itself of textural
habits which we find in Chaucer and Shakespeare,
because of the prevalent distrust of metaphor and its
reminder of the unknown areas of being. Metaphorical
life had to be restored to poetry consciously by such
writers as Keats and Hopkins. Country people, of
course, continued to practise metaphor, turning words
like "rheumatic," to "screwmatic," inventing saws and
preserving folk-poetry in their songs. These habits of
language are integral to our native way of life as is
modal folk melody. And as educated contemporary
music has made such great advances by "finding" folk
music in the last half-century, perhaps the future of
poetry lies in the restoration to the language of poetry
elements of these native habits, along with the kind of

meticulous re-exploration of the nature of metaphor and conceptual thought such as T. S. Eliot makes in *Four Quartets*.

Forby shows that in 1830 "snitered," "snart" and "snayped" were still extant in the North of England. Let us compare the local idiomatic meaning with the meaning given in the Early English Text Society Edition: *Snitered:* Yorkshire "snitter" to snow; a "snitter" is a biting blast; EETS: drove, drifted. *Snart:* Cumberland, Yorkshire "snar," "snarry," cold, piercing; EETS: severely, sharply, from old Norse "snart." *Snayped:* N. England, to check, restrain; EETS, from old English "snaip": to snub, nip, pierce.

Now in the dialect of 1830 we find that these words which, in the poem of c.1400 were live metaphor—the *snow drove* full *sharply* that *pierced* the wild (creatures)—have slipped into more hollow, dead metaphor, cliché. "Snitter" now means "to snow" or "a bitter blast" rather than "drove" or "drifted"; "snart" means "cold," rather than "sharp"; "snaip" "to check" rather than "to nip or pierce"—though these transitions have all happened in relation to the subject of cold and snow. In the process—and it could be examined in better detail by a properly qualified philologist—we see the way the natural life of language (which is always in formation and extension over new territory of experience), its vital freshness, is in metaphor, and that metaphor is an integral part of the expression, contemplation, and sharing of experience. This one can confirm by tracing any word in the language in an Etymological or the Shorter Oxford Dictionary through the ages of its use.[1] For instance "scraggy": lean, rough, has earlier meant "a weak old man" as a Swedish dialect noun (*skragga*) and in Danish *skrog* a carcase. "Wrong" can be traced back to Danish "vrang," part of the verb "to wring"; and Dutch "wrang," acid, sour ("because it wrings the mouth" says Skeat). Thus we see the name for an abstract moral quality emerge by metaphor from contact with the ordinary daily object, and the energy of physical life.

Now it is the privilege of idiomatic saw—moral statement about life—and of song and poetry, to make these metaphorical extensions of the power of language: to take a simple and common example: "She looked as though butter wouldn't melt in her mouth, but cheese would not have choked her." And we now have the expression "to butter someone up"; the use of "butter," "melt," "cheese" and "choke" here are in the simple process of metaphorical development. By metaphorical complexity in the folk-song the flower, bush, thorn became references to bodily sexual life, but also to betraying characteristics of human sexual life which are common experience: what we have here is a moral warning from communal experience:

> *I put my hand into one soft bush,*
> *Thinking the sweetest flower to find;*
> *I pricked my finger right through to the bone—*
> *I left the sweetest flower alone.*

The great qualities of Shakespeare's later plays and the writing of Bunyan and Herbert draw on these language habits of the English people: and these are enriched by the popular sermon tradition and the remarkable variegated elements of the Authorized Version. But it is the greater privilege of conscious poetry to create new metaphor—which either stands in the one poem as an extension of language, as with Shakespeare's "Or in the beached *margent* of the sea;" or words can come from poetry into the common tongue, as did Shakespeare's "ensconce" or "beggared," from

> *Against that time do I* ensconce *me here*
> *Within the knowledge of mine own desert.*
> SONNET xlix.

> *It* beggar'd *all description.*
> ANTONY & CLEOPATRA.

The word "sneap" as meaning "nip or pinch with cold," is freshly used in *The Winter's Tale* to mean "cold, blighting" (winds of rumour):

> of what may chance
> Or breed upon our absence: that may blow
> No sneaping winds at home . . .
>
> THE WINTER'S TALE I. ii. 12.

Now "sneap" here takes us on from considering metaphor to consider further qualities of the texture of words, and back to our line from *Sir Gawaine*. Sneap is allied to "snub"; Skeat traces it back through E "sneap" to pinch, Icelandic "sneypa" to castrate (*or* disgrace or snub—a significant connection), Swedish "snopa" to castrate, Danish dialect *sneve* to dock, to snub, to nip. So that for the word "sneap" to mean "pinched by the cold" we have almost a recollection of something like the cliché jest about freezing the testicles off a brass monkey. In the Northern Countries the loss of fingers and nose might well be a physical fact in the cold—cf. snub-nosed, and the word *sneap* here enacts two things —a mouth-movement of *distaste*—of antipathy to cold, which has by metaphor remained in "snub," "sneak" and such words, so that the word has *tone* (which Shakespeare is making use of in Polixenes' speech to suggest his distaste for rumour and comment of an irresponsible and dangerous kind for a ruler) — expressive of attitudes towards. And, also, a muscular movement of the talking organ associated with physical pain, of the "being-nipped" sort.

At this point, I want to requote our line and turn to the theories of language of Sir Richard Paget: "The snawë snitered ful snart, that snayped the wyldë." And let us bear in mind Shakespeare's "sneap" which is obviously linked with "snayped," and turn to Sir Richard Paget on mouth gesture:

Gesturally SN—is very similar to ST—and SL. The tongue tip performs almost exactly the same backward movement, but with this difference, that . . . in SN— the tongue tip and its edges make a complete *continuing* closure right across the mouth. SN—would therefore appear to be a more substantial and enduring drawing-in gesture than SL . . . *Snow*—old English SNAW— rather suggests a fine textured material (S), held high up (N) or which drifts (SN) instead of outwards (W). The Red Indians and deaf mutes both use lateral ges-tures of their hands to represent snow falling . . . re-viewing the words in SN—it will be found that they all refer to drawing in or up, or projecting . . . It has long been known that there was a relationship between SN— and the human nose . . . our study of tongue gesture which produced the sound of SN—makes the relation-ship clear; indeed we find that of 34 short English words 29 i.e. 85 per cent are clearly gestural . . .

THIS ENGLISH.

Sir Richard Paget suggests a complexity of gestural tongue movements which *enact* the character of the referent of each SN—word. To add to what he says about snow, the soft "S" sound is followed by a closed nasal sound above the continuing closure right across the mouth on N enacting the full sky from which the snow descends ("Coldë clengeth adoun" is another phrase from *Sir Gawaine*), which it does with A or O and W. With a long O or A vowel the mouth movement after SN—suggests the drifting or escaping force of snow. But with the shorter vowel there is a kind of facial nut-cracker feeling in the combination of consonants, by which the nose is wrinkled (as in sneer, snarl, sneeze, snare). There is the closed nasal noise, and this is followed by a rapid projection of the tongue downwards away from the palate, which movement is accompanied by a feeling of slight coolness as the breath passes the tip of the tongue. Thus words beginning in SN—are those concerned with derision (sneer, sneak) with the nose (snout, snook, snuff, sneeze), with projecting things (snag, snood), with pincer movements (snip, snap) and with the pains in the extremities by extreme cold (snub, sneap). A *snake* and a *snail* are both things like a projecting limb, and things one fears, or despises out of fear, or contempt: they are cold to the touch like an exposed member.

Of course, one can go on exploring possibilities of language gesture: the problem is to stop at what is relevant. What seems to me relevant here is that *"sneap" enacts*, in the very nature of its form as a gesture in the speaking organ, the pinching nip of cold, the expression of distaste for cold, and the fear for the extremities in cold (lodged far back in its original meaning of castration). And this enactment is an important element in our language, certainly in words from Anglo-Saxon. "The snawë snitered ful snart, that snayped the wyldë" then, as a line of poetry, enacts as you read it aloud (or if you don't you will vestigially remember the mouth movements: though it is possible that silent reading has a lot to do with our increasing insensitivity to language) —the line enacts the sneaping effects of the cold: "snitered" giving the texture of "bite" or "bitter" to snow, "snart" giving it sharpness, and "snayped" giving the fear-of-frostbitten-limbs seen sympathetically in the wretched wild animals. Much of these flavours of sound come to us still from the traditional textural habits of English: how easy it is, when it is read aloud, for ordinary people to recapture the flavour of *Sir Gawaine*, 600 years later!

It is this in-the-mouth texture of language in poetry which adds *movement*—the feel of outward or inward physical, muscular, blood experience embodied in words. In our line, for instance, the fear of the winter cold is there in the contemptuous nose-wrinkling SN consonant.

Cloudes kesten kenly the colde to the earth
With nye enough of the north the naked to tene
   [tene = grieve]
The snawe snitered ful snart, that snayped the wylde
The werbelande wynd wapped fro the hygh. .
And drof each dale ful of dryftes ful grete.

Now I think it is not perverse of me to use a passage from *Sir Gawaine*. The art of one epoch, as Mr. Eliot reminds us, does not superannuate the art of any previous one, and what we have in this poetry is the essence of the use of language in English poetry. These language habits have gone on developing: we inherit them. "Sneap" has gone, but the "SN" gesture of contempt (*snob, snide, snag*), of pincer-movement (*snack, snare, snatch, snood*), of having-to-do-with-the-nose (*snuff, snipe*) in the texture of language has not, and many aspects of the effects of language texture are the same as they were in the fourteenth century. I take this line from 600 years ago to emphasize that what I am saying about metaphor in poetry is not some theory based on a new-fangled development in contemporary poetry. We take on English, willy-nilly with its peculiar habits, and "English must be kept up." Indeed I am really complaining that contemporary poetry has too much cut itself away from this true voice of poetry, and that Dylan Thomas's much applauded use of language *is* new-fangled and with too little roots in our 600 years of poetic history. A collection of new poets (*New Lines*) published a few years ago even went so far as to issue a denial that poetry "need be metaphorical." It must be: and what I *am* saying is that *poetry does what it says:* we do not just "take the meaning"—we possess the poem, in our nerves and blood, as well as in our intellect, at the intuitive level. That is if it *is* poetry, a form of metaphor itself. And the basis of metaphor is the need we all have, such as I have outlined, to explore reality at that intuitive level

—a process which is felt so deeply that the expression of it inevitably bears the texture of states of bodily condition, excitement, movement, and "voice."

If we take further examples of poetry whose texture enacts the meaning, we find more and more that the textural enactment embodies (and springs from) this impulse—the impulse to explore reality and then ask the philosophical question, How to live?—and seek answers in terms of whole living.

As touchstones to exemplify my requirement of living texture one may take the more memorable phrases which slide into one's head. If we remember, on a frosty morning, Coleridge's "The secret ministry of frost," our first feeling is one of intense pleasure, in that the experience we recognize is one *which we share with other human beings*: the texture (given by the conjunction of "cr," "st" and "fr" with light vowels) is that of walking on crisp frost. "Ministry" suggests the assumption of white garments, as the trees have done (nurses, accolytes "minister"): and the "secret" suggests the mysterious way in which all details of the natural scene have had, as it were, a devoted attention in being covered with hoar. The line extends our experience of any frosty morning, because it enlarges our capacity for wonder at the magic of our atmospheric environment: "ministry" and "secret" involve us in the awe.

Awe is a moral condition, here brought about by the metaphorical activity of the phrase, an important moral condition because it leads us away from arrogance into humility, and brings us to better terms with ourselves, with the consequent chastening of our more self-assertive potentialities. Such, of course, culminate in public terms in such manifestations as the hydrogen bomb, reckless disposal of radio-active waste, disturbance of natural patterns of fauna, soil erosion, assassination, and such consequences of our shared moral weaknesses. In personal terms our lack of humility may cause forms of aggression or attempts at domination, and consequent suffering. Personal order is necessary for social order. The quality of language used as poetry is as important as these issues are serious human ones: to be irresponsible about language is to be irresponsible about man's inward conflict with his own infirm nature, and his contest with external nature. To abrogate our responsibilities to the word is to abrogate our responsibilities as men living in a natural world, ourselves natural creatures.

To reinforce the argument we may take some lines of Shakespeare's. Here is the Duke of Albany talking to his wife Goneril:

> You are not worth the dust which the rude wind
> Blows in your face. I fear your disposition:
> That nature which condemns its origin
> Cannot be bordered certain in itself;
> She that herself will sliver and disbranch
> From her material sap, perforce must wither,
> And come to deadly use.
>
> KING LEAR, Act IV, Sc. ii.

I suppose I can hardly claim that these lines came to me at random, at a time when I was pondering the relevance of poetry to such human issues as I mention above. From a dramatic poem on the nature of man and of nature they bear a direct relation to them. But, of course, we recall them so readily because they have the authority of the delight and wisdom from which they sprang. Their metaphorical power here resides in the submerged image of man-as-a-tree-or-plant. Though everything is founded on it, the image itself is hardly given explicitly, yet it is itself a symbolic contemplation of man's nature in nature. The metaphorical force is thus at one with a deep philosophical con-

sideration: what is man, and how can he live? Without
such deep moral concern about the nature of man and
the natural reality he inhabits, such delightful poetry
could never have been written.

We experience delight in the texture and substance
of "sliver and disbranch." These words give us, in the
saying (or hearing) the feel in the mouth-muscles of
working in green wood, tearing and paring away shoots,
lopping off branches: *sliver* is the texture and movement of slipping off small growths, *disbranch* those of
using axe, cleaver or wedge on cellular-textured wood.
As we experience these work-feelings, so we are brought
to feel the sap of which the tree is created (*material*)
exposed, and come to mere *deadly use* (not growth).
The metaphor is exactly that of those forms of treatment of growth that lead to, say, soil-erosion as caused
by ring-barking trees: but as Albany is talking of
Goneril the process is taken by us as one in the human
spirit, which inevitably leads to such external denatur-
ings.

By our sensory relish in the tactile and movement
forces of the language we enter into, or possess, both
Albany's condemnation of such unnaturalness, and
Goneril's impulses to denature herself. We are thus
brought to experience Shakespeare's experience of Albany and Goneril—and thus moral conflict is being
enacted in our own breasts, as well as the poet's. The
process of the plant growing out of the dust which is
worthless and blows in our faces, then spoiling itself,
withering, and coming only to deadly uses echoes the
stoical contemplation of life in popular sayings
("thou'lt never be satisfied till thou gets thy mouth full
of mould"), and the poetic realism of the Psalms. Yet
it conveys too the additional force of Shakespeare's
own grasp on life, his positive moral concern. He makes
Goneril's reply significantly full of emptiness:

France spreads her banners in our noiseless land . . .
Whiles thou a moral fool, sitst still and criest
'Alack, why does he so?'

In full maturity the responsible poet may attain an assurance of voice which has itself a metaphorical power—taking us into his confidence in human nature —something we could never have attained ourselves. These lines, for instance, have the very movement of sincerity, and the rhythm of perfect, but unattainable, order in human love:

> *What you do*
> *Still betters what is done. When you speak, sweet*
> *I'ld have you do it ever: when you sing,*
> *I'ld have you buy and sell so; so give alms;*
> *Pray so; and, for the ord'ring your affairs,*
> *To sing them too: when you do dance, I wish you*
> *A wave o' the sea, that you might ever do*
> *Nothing but that; move still, still so,*
> *And own no other function . . .*
>
> THE WINTER'S TALE, Act IV, Sc. iii

The underlying awareness of time, change, death, the rhythms and patterns of life here is profound; but it expresses itself by the simplest of ways of handling language; "move still, still so" where the shape of the wave and its movement is given in the repetition and in the vowel sounds, while the fact that the word repeated is "still" gives both the yearned-after timelessness and statuesqueness (from the ambiguity of "still" which meant both "always" and "quiet") which the "wave of the sea" suggests is impossible: the sea is never still, there is no unique everlasting wave as the Prince wishes Perdita to be, but only always incessant innumerable waves. The wish of the lover for permanent timeless perfection itself thrusts her into the perspective of numberless humanity and infinite time. Such are the

unseen depths of awareness beneath the innocent
simplicity of this verse's movement. The simplicity and
absolute acceptance of man's tragic reality achieved at
the end of *King Lear* is behind this verse. The wisdom
of the *Sonnets* and the Tragedies is embodied in its
movement.

Or one may take any of the following random pieces,
to explore the relationship between metaphor, texture
and moral attitude:

> *What I had seen*
> *Of grey cathedrals, buttress's walls, rent towers,*
> *The superannuation of sunk realms,*
> *Or Nature's rocks toil'd hard in waves and winds,*
> *Seems but the faulture of decrepit things*
> *To that eternal domed monument.*
>
> JOHN KEATS.

> *There fed by food they love, to rankest size*
> *Around the dwellings docks and wormwood rise;*
> *Here the strong mallow strikes her slimy root,*
> *Here the dull nightshade hangs her deadly fruit.*
>
> GEORGE CRABBE.

> *Strike, churl; hurl cheerless wind, then; heltering hail*
> *May's beauty massacre and wisped wild clouds grow*
> *Out on the giant air; tell Summer No,*
> *Bid joy back, have at the harvest, keep Hope pale,*
>
> GERARD MANLEY HOPKINS.

> *First, the cold friction of expiring sense*
> *Without enchantment, offering no promise*
> *But bitter tastelessness of shadow fruit*
> *As body and soul begin to fall asunder,*
>
> T. S. ELIOT.

> *Surely among a rich man's flowering lawns,*
> *Amid the rustle of his planted hills*
> *Life overflows without ambitious pains;*
> *And rains down life until the basin spills . . .*
>
> W. B. YEATS.

In each of these, one could discuss that texture, that feel-in-the mouth of the pondering of reality, of ordered attitudes-towards, which is the voice of true poetry. I am suggesting that the finest texture of language in poetry depends, in the end, on an impulse towards truth, a more effective dealing with reality, and a deeper sense of integration and order. Eliot's "But bitter tastelessness" enacts the spitting out of a rejected form of life; Yeats's "Until the basin spills," with its "open" sounds—"among," "flowering," "planted"—enacts a yearned-for ease, ceremony and plenty culminating in the overflowing labial "l's" in the last line; in Crabbe's "Strikes" a "*slimy* root" we have two conflicting attitudes embodied in language, of disgust for the common weed, and admiration for its courage and energy, which relates to the poet's feelings of sympathy with the poor humanity whose dwellings the weeds surround: they too—as aspects of the human reality which troubled Crabbe—are wild and lead an ugly life, but have vigour. And Keats's abstract "superannuation," "faulture," "decrepit" derive a new substance from the "rent towers," "rocks toil'd hard in waves and winds," "buttress'd walls" which have a muscular solidity as we say the words (Keats has learnt his lesson from "The multitudinous seas incarnadine, / Making the green one red"). The texture of Keat's lines enacts his moral exploration of human life in time, and the nature of art itself, as a form of man-made reality.

I do not claim to have exhausted in one short chapter all kinds of poetry. Nor do I expect to in this book. I seek only to demonstrate one point. I am trying to produce touchstones to show something of what I feel true poetry must be, essentially metaphorical, concerned with the extension and deepening of our reality sense and with gaining effective hold on life. Without this impulse to explore and extend our understanding, to increase insight and develop attitudes to life, to extend the ranges of the spirit, poetry which has life in its texture, rhythms, sound, movement, cannot be written. For the vitality of its texture—the true voice of poetry—is inseparable from the metaphorical life of its language which springs from the impulse to understand life better and come to terms with it. Folk-idiom, folk-song, folk-drama and children's poetry all have these qualities because the innocent works directly from the unconscious. The poet must train himself to cooperate with unconscious phantasy and to express the intuitive apprehension in language which has life. This requires a profound sense of metaphorical responsibility.

3 CRITICAL SELF-DECEPTION

THE RECENT COLLECTION of essays on Dylan Thomas edited by Professor Tedlock has demonstrated how various are the several critics who have been disarmed by his appeal, and who have even gone so far as to aver variously that he uses language in different ways from all other writers. I contest this special allowance for Thomas's use of language, and suggest that one of our problems with this poet is that we have been too much disarmed by his appeal, even to the extent of failing to see the consequences of the metaphorical irresponsibility of which I accuse him.

I propose here to examine the arguments of a representative critic of the work of Dylan Thomas, because at the centre of his arguments lies the contention that we should accept Thomas's poetry as not metaphorical at all, but operating by what he calls "symbols." What seems to me evident is that in order to accept Dylan Thomas's poetry at all we have to inhibit all our normal responses to the language, and particularly to those metaphorical processes of language which are the very life of language itself. In doing this we do not find our perceptions enlarged, but, rather, baffled.

These are Professor Olson's arguments in his main

chapter, roughly indicated by brief quotations (I don't
think I travesty):

> How seriously are we to take the poet's insistence
> that his poetry be read literally? . . . [he then quotes
> some lines] . . . this is scarcely literal language . . . Is
> it then metaphorical? [no] In short we have here not
> metaphor, but symbolism . . . why should Thomas
> have couched his poetry in symbols so esoteric? . . . A
> symbol . . . exhibits something to us as an actuality,
> and so affects us more strongly [than metaphor and
> simile which are "figures of speech"] . . . Thomas's use
> of symbols must be judged in terms of its effectiveness
> in the individual poem . . . what is likely to strike his
> reader first of all is Thomas's extraordinary *conception*
> of these themes [of birth, life, love and death] . . . his
> poetic imagination transports him into the mysteries of
> the womb . . . he employs symbols to coerce the
> imagination . . . to build as very real indeed a fan-
> tastic universe of his own . . . Is it not a Grand Guig-
> nol theatre? Is it not all stage magic and melodrama?
> The plucking out of eyes is horrible. Not so in tragedy:
> the event takes on its character from its happening to
> the tragic figure . . . there can be no tragedy if we do
> not value the characters highly . . . the essence of
> tragedy is that its action must embody grave and uni-
> versal truths. Thomas shows us that to a serious and
> sensitive individual, life in the absence of a sustaining
> faith is a nightmare, and so it is; and if that nightmare
> is as horrible . . . images which adumbrate that horrow
> do not exaggerate it—they express it. Without their
> reference, the symbols of Thomas would be melodra-
> matic, even morbid; because they have reference to the
> serious suffering of a man of some nobility, they are
> tragic.

There seem to me here extraordinary deficiencies in
the critical logic: and these are due to a particular kind
of critical abandon which nearly always occurs in

critical writing about this "most unintellectual of our poets" (Henry Treece). The fact is that there is in Thomas's poetry a power to charm, drug, and to disarm, in such a way as to drive critics like Olson to seek to explain away conclusions of their own which, allowed to progress, would reduce Thomas's claims to recognition to very small proportions. How does this happen?

Significantly, once he abandons the attempt to argue cogently against objections to Dylan Thomas's faults, Olson lapses into a *hwyl* [1] of his own:

> These are tokens of a mighty, an appalling imagination that sweeps us up with it, like an angel, and forces us to endure the visions of another world, thronged with enchantments and horrors . . .
>
> It is a nightmare universe, a universe of darkness and fright, a world under the 'forever falling night' of time; a world unsaved by Christ, and unsaveable, doomed.

The critic so shares the indulgence in the emotional satisfactions of doom and horror, that he cannot coolly read his own argument.

His argument, in so far as it is consecutive at all (it is some kind of circular argument), depends on our accepting that Dylan Thomas's poetry is "tragic" rather than "melodramatic" *because the poet himself is noble*. Does this mean in his person, or in the poetical "I" of the poetry? If the first, how does the writer know and on what does he base his assumption (in the personal life there seemed almost to be a cultivation of the ignoble)? If the second—and it can surely only be the second—as what one most relevantly wants to know of a poet is through the communication of his work—then how is the nobility distinguishable from—how can it be distinguished from—the created "nightmare"? Even if this poet separates himself as "Marlais" or "Mr. Thomas" he never achieves an impersonal dramatic central figure such as Gerontion in Mr. Eliot's poem.

The "noble" self of the child is all too present insistently in the "nightmare"—its presence is indeed, the only reason we are willing to accept it. This explains Mr. Olson's circular argument. But can one ever accept the argument at all that *it is the nobility of the author that makes for tragedy?* Even if one accepts the conventional Aristotelian argument that it is the tragic figure's nobility which makes tragedy, whoever suggested that the *author's* nobility had anything to do with it? Is *Lear* a tragedy because Shakespeare was noble? Of course, the poet has to convince us of the nobility of his created characters: which, of course, presupposes that he is capable of conceiving nobility. But this is not to be confused with his "own" nobility.

The secret of Dylan Thomas's hypnotic disarming effect is that he manages to convince us of his nobility, because he insists on our taking his expression as that of the infant, outside normal adult moral considerations, as of the omnipotent child who demands total approval. His poems emerge from the "tumultuous world of my own being" and to fail to respond to the self-imputed nobility is to offer an offence, at the deeper level, to the infant self—an offence we are intuitively inhibited from giving, as to a child.

This self-attributed nobility emerges from a desperate need on Thomas's part to be regarded by his audience as an infant is regarded by his all-pardoning, unconditionally loving, mother. This appeal operates through the language Thomas devised to conduct his astonishing ploy on his readers. But the impulse is deficient in reality-sense: it is always anxious and always defensively egocentric because an adult cannot be a child, and a child's relationship with reality and other people could only be a limitation on adult living. This will be argued in detail below. But this disarming influence of Thomas's very language explains how such a critic as Professor Olson can deceive himself—a defensive mechanism, it demands tolerance, and invokes the attitude of "like an angel."

Surely one cannot make the exploration of unusual ranges of experience an excuse for evading the poet's responsibility to language? He can surely only arrive at such unusual ranges by greater responsibility? And if symbols "exhibit to us actualities" how can they do so except by "figures of speech"? What else, *other* than words and figures can convey "symbols"? Perhaps Mr. Olson has been taught too rigidly at school that metaphors, like similes, are "figures of speech," like plums in the cake: additions, rather than the very fibre of all language? He says Dylan Thomas's poetry is not metaphorical: but surely the vitality of language is essentially in metaphor, and the extension of language over new ranges of experience can only be by way of metaphor? How can symbols exist in poetry apart from the figures of words, the metaphorical medium by which they are expressed—except they be drawn on the page as pictures?

Mr. Olson reveals how unsatisfactory is his conception of metaphor in his contribution to the symposium *Dylan Thomas, the Legend and the Poet*—in poetry the proper function of metaphor is apparently to be "left aside":

> The point in employing any literary device is that in the circumstances it discharges its function better than any other. Metaphor and simile, for instance (if we leave aside their instructive functions of making the unfamiliar known in terms of the familiar), have two principal functions in poetry: either they isolate a quality or qualities by indicating something else which has them, or they serve as an indication of thought, feeling, or character; and it is thus that the poet controls the feelings and ideas of his reader. When Enobarbus says

that Cleopatra's barge 'burnt' on the water, its fire-like brilliance is singled out: when Hamlet calls the world 'a rank, unweeded garden' he manifests his state of mind. Both kinds fail, of course, if no real or fancied resemblance can be found to justify the analogy; but the former kind fails in its special function when the qualities isolated are, either in kind or degree, insufficient to produce the idea which might be grasped or the emotion which must be felt; and the latter kind fails in its special function when it fails to identify thought, feeling, or character.

Significantly, Olson misses the deeper meaning of Shakespeare's "burnt"—the consuming sensuality of Cleopatra (cf. "and what they undid, did" which enacts the moving fans whose sensuousness "undoes" by consuming). The "instructive functions" as Olson calls them *cannot* be left aside—this *is* how language works.

The confusion is common though one would think the facts simple enough. When we read, we read words which always function metaphorically—they do not have a "special" function in poetry, even if they have finer functions. How can symbols affect us more strongly (as "actualities") than by the metaphor and simile—the word—by which we apprehend the symbols? [2]

Olson has naively brought himself into an extraordinary dichotomy between language and symbol. But we shall see soon what he does mean. Take the lines he offers as the "token of a mighty, an appalling imagination," and we shall see that really Olson is making apologies for the lack of genuine poetic texture, for he partly sees that Dylan Thomas's work gives the appearance of poetry without living substance—it is in fact largely the product of studied and practised deceptions. Olson joins in the plea for a special mask-language. Yet much of Dylan Thomas is meaningless.

In the beginning was the mounting fire
That set alight the weathers from a spark,
A three-eyed, red-eyed spark, blunt as a flower;
Life rose and spouted from the rolling seas,
Burst in the roots, pumped from the earth and rock
The secret oils that drive the grass.

Of course one can see this is vaguely, and in a common place way, about phallic creation (the "red-eyed" phallus of God "mounting" chaos and setting alight the weathers by a spark of God's substance). But one demands from poetry (unless our conception of poetry be meaningless) a use of figurative elements that is impelled to explore fresh aspects of reality, and thus come alive in the contributing elements of the language. Also, poetry has its logic; and good poetry must first be good prose—Dylan Thomas achieved a method of defying these requirements in order to delude the reader into believing that he has before him some "new" form of poetry. This is sometimes concealed by a great deal of extravagant surrealist theory about the "autonomy of the symbol" and so forth.

Let me compare a poet with whom Dylan Thomas is sometimes unfortunately equated. Dylan Thomas uses Hopkins's rhythms and phrases often to add to his work a suggestion of Hopkins's religious ecstasy, as in *In Country Sleep:*

> *. . . And high, there, on the hare—*
>   *Heeled winds the rooks*
> *Cawing from their black bethels soaring, the holy*
>   *books*
> *Of birds . . .*

For him Hopkins was the model for kinds of breathless recklessness: Hopkins's language is always in fact in perfect control:

> *Delightfully the bright wind boisterous ropes, wres-*
>   *tles, beats earth bare*

Of yestertempest's creases; in pool and rut peel
parches
Squandering ooze to squeezed dough, crust, dust;
stanches, starches
Squadroned masks and manmarks treadmire toil
there
Footfretted in it. Million-fuelèd nature's bonfire
burns on.
But quench her bonniest, dearest to her, her clearest-
selvèd spark
Man, how fast his firedint, his mark on mind, is
gone!
Both are in an unfathomable, all is in an enormous
dark
Drowned . . .

>   *That Nature is a Heraclitean fire*
>   *and of the Comfort of the Resurrection.*

I take these lines in case I am supposed to be
objecting to Dylan Thomas's poetry from the grounds
of some "literary decorum." Hopkins's lines have the
oddity to which he himself confessed ("it is the vice of
distinctiveness to become queer. This vice I cannot
have escaped"), and normal syntax is over-ridden. Yet
essentially the lines are "good prose": the compressions
and elisions are a development of normal syntax, not an
abandoning of syntax altogether. The subject of the
verbs "ropes, wrestles, beats" is the boisterous wind (cf.
"Wroth wind of the welkyn wrasteleth with the sunne"
in *Sir Gawaine and the Grene Knight*). It is the wind,
too, which in "pool and rut-peel" "peel-parches squandering ooze"—that is, dries up the puddles, pools, and
squeezed ribbons of mud in the lanes—which peel as
they dry because of the different consistencies of mud,
and the leaves and other fragments mixed in it ("peel,"
that is, operates as both noun and adverb). The wind,
too, "stanches" (an archaic form of "staunches"—
"staunch" presumably suppressed because of the sug-

gestion of blood, not here invoked, and "stanch" preferred because of its flavour or movement associated with the ambiguous suggestion of "stanchion," a post, pillar, or prop—that is, of fixing into solidity) and "starches" the trodden mud into "masks"—the hard fixed image of people's efforts trailing backwards and forwards in it. "Squadroned" because the marks made by a few look like the footmarks of a squadron of hundreds of men, marching in order. "Treadmire toil there foot fretted in it": the toil of people treading in the mire is there embossed and chequered in the squandering ooze, now "crust, dust."

There is nothing in those lines, in fact, which stands outside the range of "good prose," although liberties are taken with normal syntax. What liberties are taken are taken to good effect—to give us in the texture of the language a man's relish for the changing patterns of nature, which fixes the "manmarks" within its "squadroned masks." "Ropes, wrestles, beats" are *metaphorical enactments* of the force of the wind as felt by men: "starches, dough, crust," suggests the intimacy between man's daily life and death and natural phenomena. So by the metaphorical vitality of language, the onomatopoeia ("squandering ooze to squeezed"), and the movement ("squandering . . . squadroned"—where the "squ . . . d" movement of the speaking voice, enacting the squelching of liquid mud, comes suddenly first upon "stanches" "starches" and then the harder "d" of "squad," which gives in the larynx and mouth the physical feel of the change, during the windy day, in the texture of the mud) —we possess the presence of Man in Nature. Thus the argument which follows is given a felt substance—"but once quench man, how fast the mark he makes by his fire on nature, how fast his mark on mind would be gone from the earth. Both, nature and man, would be in an unfathom-

able . . . no, *everything* would be drowned in an
enormous dark." Yet this is no simple prose logic, for
"firedint" suggests not only man's mark made by an
effort or blow, but also a spark from a flint as though
man's existence on earth were as brief as a spark from a
struck flint. That image from man's ability to make fire
suggests the immense contrast between Nature's
million-fuelèd bonfire—the sun and all energy derived
from it—and man's own puny firedint, which yet gives
everything its significance.

Now all the things seen, felt and *thought* in these
lines, "symbols" as they may be, derive entirely from
the vitality of the language, from "figures of speech,"
from words, from metaphor, and the textural enactment which conveys the strength and vitality of Hopkins's exploration of the nature of man in his reality.
How could there be anything else there other than
figures of speech, words on the page, sounds, echoes
from the English tongue? Only through such figures
(or tricks) of speech as "treadmire toil there footfretted in it," with its verbal suggestions of treadmill,
quagmire; and the "foot fretted" alliteration and character of word giving not only the pattern of the
embossed mud, but the sound and feeling in the
mouth of feet in the mud, enacting toil and fret. The
struggle with the figures of speech was for Hopkins a
struggle to impose a pattern on experience: and the
vitality of his lines is the vitality of a moral concern
associated with this struggle for order. Hopkins has
given body and form to the Heraclitean philosophy of
flux, in some conflict with his Jesuitical training, in
apprehending man's place in the universe.

To return to Dylan Thomas's lines is to return to the
imitation of poetry, to Llareggub language. To understand his lines at all one needs (*and this is what Mr.
Olson is virtually saying*) to inhibit all one's normal

relish for language. One has to cut oneself off from the inheritance, from the pressure of traditional ambiguity and texture in the life of every English word. It is a normal part of the process of responding to poetry to share the poet's attempt to define by excluding unnecessary or irrelevant associations: Hopkins's "squadroned" is nowadays less successful than it was for him, because of new flavours of the word (aircraft, uniforms, tanks) which we must suppress. But Hopkins is weak in such ways sometimes because of isolation, not irresponsibility. Dylan Thomas, however, could have had no reason to suppose that "Pumped from the earth and rock / The secret oils that drive the grass" would not suggest mineral oils, like petrol, which are "pumped from the earth and rock" and "drive" things. Here we must take "oil" not as a word with its Biblical associations (which "In the beginning" might lead us to expect) of anointment; or with its sense of "secret oils" in food; or poppy; or even hormones; or with its advertisement sense of "secret oils" for use in cars—not as the word in everyday use (cf. Hopkins's "starch" "crust" "dough") but in some one special symbolic sense belonging to the poet's own esoteric symbolism.

Again "drive" does not here convey the force of nature, because it lies on the page uncontrolled by its companions: "nature's bonfire burns on" has the homogeneity of the organic metaphorical life of language: a bonfire burns organic matter. There is some force in Dylan Thomas's "mounting fire" (that "set alight the weathers"), but when examined—to see if it be good prose—this feels less substantial: for if the weathers were there to be set alight, then they had already been created—the weakness is in the realization of the process. The sexual sense of "mount" does not tie in organically with "weathers." It is not a matter of the writer being "unintellectual," but of the writer not having the faculty of being able to use language in poetry. The words here did not grow from the deeper centres—they have been manhandled externally. Hopkins gives us the exact features of Nature's bonfire by taking some few aspects of its million-fuelèd hugeness, and bringing them to our senses in a complex felt way: and, as I hope I have shown, this is not simply a matter of imagery. Our response to "A three-eyed, red-eyed spark, blunt as a flower" cannot even be that of allowing an image to form. Perhaps (who can tell?) the three eyes are those of the Trinity (one could permit the omission of "pairs")? "Redeyed" is a cliché expression of optical exhaustion by fatigue, anger or drink: but how can a "spark" have eyes? A spark could *be* an eye. "Redeyed" may suggest a penis, but how can a penis be a "spark," since the phrase is "red-eyed spark"? "Blunt as a flower" it is impossible to see, grasp or realize, as "blunt" suggests a tactual strength of resistance to cutting or striking or piercing (cf. "blunt instrument"): the sullen texture of "blunt" is difficult to reconcile with "flower." "Flowers" are conventionally fragile, some are phallic and can thrust, cleave, and "take the winds of March with beauty": flowers *can* have an attributed substantiality in poetry, but here we are at a loss to know which substantiality is meant— visual, fallaciously pathetic, or tactile. (Derek Stanford, in his book on Dylan Thomas, says this is an apocalyptic phallus, but are we prepared to take the confusion of "mounting," setting alight, rising, and spouting as offering anything but commonplace "surrealist" gesture at "genesis"?)

If we pay closer attention than vague blurred response we find that such a phrase as "burst in the roots" suggests a force bursting roots, or among the roots, or the roots themselves bursting as plants burst when they are stimulated by "hormone" poisons. The traditional textural activity of the word "burst" with its plosive consonant, here, needs to be inhibited, and the word's meaning confined to the cliché activity it has in "I'm bursting with energy"—one can only respond to this poetry by impoverishing one's response to language. We are not led to a new "fantastic universe," but into the impotent confusion of an "apocalyptic banter."

The movement and rhythm of these lines, as compared with the lines of Hopkins, is as poor as the use of language: it merely mimics, stands instead of, genuine rhythm in poetry. "Burst," "pump," "drive" give only the movement of the urging grunt, the wishing to express something astonishingly apocalyptic. Hopkins's movement convinces us of the acute sensitivity, aliveness, of his mind and senses. Thomas's flat last line convinces us only of his failure to fly.

The comparison of these two pieces of verse reveals the weaknesses at the heart of Dylan Thomas's writing, as of much of the poetry accumulated in books of contemporary verse. It is essentially not metaphorical. To respond to Dylan Thomas's verse the reader has to limit his response to *cliché*—poetic cliché maybe, but cliché none the less. That is, the reader will *not* hold his ears, his palate and nerves, keenly alert to the fullest range of metaphor, sound, pattern, texture, movement. He will greet each word on its own, to the exclusion of its fellows, and take it according to some one special meaning allotted to it by the poet. Except, that is for some phrases such as "In the beginning" to which the reader is expected to respond with the fullest and widest (but vague) surge of feeling, and except for other whimsical verbal manipulations such as "all the moon long" or "happy as the grass was green" to which, irrespective of the predominant mood or tenour of the poem in question, he will be expected to respond with delight as "striking" phrases in themselves.

The following are some further conclusions of Mr. Olson's:

> In the last period adjective is piled on adjective, masses of words are jammed together to make one compound epithet, until the ordinary reader can scarcely stretch his breath over the long reaches of language. Despite the enchanting imagery, one has the feeling that eloquence is sometimes strained . . . curiously enough he never achieves lucidity: the obscurity wrought by his early terseness slips into the obscurity wrought by his final verbosity . . . [p. 21.]
>
> Perhaps he becomes a bit too consciously the bard overwhelming us with his copiousness of language, his eloquence, booming at us, working upon us too obviously, even exciting himself unnecessarily. I do not find him melodramatic in his early poems: but I confess there is some foundation for supposing him sentimental in his last. It is not that one would rather not have had these poems: one would rather have had them better . . . [p. 22.]
>
> Moved by grief for a burned child (in A Refusal to Mourn), nobly and powerfully moved as he is, he does not suffer imaginatively the experience of the child, does not share in it in the least: he sees the pain and the horror from without, and the resolution he reaches is for him, not the child. This curiously external view is revealed in one of his least successful poems: the death of a hundred year old man provides him matter for a string of fantastic conceits, and the poem is really unintelligible, not because it is particularly obscure, but because the emotion he exhibits is impossible to relate to any emotion that the event, however conceived, conceived if you will from the point of view of a man from Mars could have aroused in us. I have remarked, indeed argued, that Thomas's imagination could trans-

port him anywhere, through all space and all time: but it is also true that, wherever it takes him, he sees nothing but himself . . . [p. 23.]

After these passages, which would be sufficient one would have thought to establish the writer as lacking in the essential qualities of a poet—care with language, and power of compassion—Olson goes on to say "he is a Keats, a Byron, a Yeats, or an Eliot . . . these two limitations—his restriction to certain ranges of emotion, and his restriction to one character—must not be taken seriously, for they amount to this: that he was a lyric poet of the lofty kind . . . I am not, I hope the reader will understand, concerned with Thomas's faults . . . I am also not trying to legislate . . ." Then Olson descends into some more undigested Aristotelian-ism about pity, fear, and evaluation, and recommends us to read "Twenty-four Years," "Poem in October" and "Poem on his Birthday." These—the work of the "lyric poet of the lofty kind"—will apparently stifle criticism. "Legislation" has been disarmed by the very intensity of Thomas's appeal—that one must not legislate against the infant.

Dylan Thomas himself, of course, shows little capacity for self-criticism, except in a few poems (see Chapter 6). His appeal consists in the calculated disarming irresponsibility—the child's amoral attitude to its expression. In introducing his works he affects this casual irresponsibility: "to choose what I should read tonight, I looked through seventy odd poems of mine, and found that many *are* odd indeed and that some may be poems . . ." His earlier poems he says "have a vehement beat pounding black and green rhythms like those of a very young policeman exploding." Such impish avowal of irresponsibility is part of his stock in trade: it disarms criticism and is part of the mask.

With the casual air goes a determined romantic pose, intended to make criticism a personal offence to the appealing infant.

> This is the only one I have written that is, directly, about the life and death of one particular human being I knew—and not about the very many lives and deaths whether seen, as in my first poems, *in the tumultuous world of my own being* . . . [italics supplied]

This defensive egotism Dylan Thomas made his advantage, and his wide popularity depends upon the combination of the attitude "take it or leave it," with the petulant "but it's from my tumultuous soul all the same." A similar egotism is the mark of much present day writing by younger poets.

The poem in question, *After the Funeral*, "about one particular human being," contains these lines:

> *I stand, for this memorial's sakes, alone*
> *In the snivelling hours with dead, humped Ann* . . .
> *But I, Ann's bard on a raised hearth, call all*
> *The seas to service that her wood-tongued virtue*
> *Babble like a bellbuoy* . . .
> *Storm me forever over her grave* . . .

And, whoever Ann was, we feel like Hamlet, who protested: "What is he whose grief / Bears such an emphasis?"

Professor Olson is a representative critic of Dylan Thomas who does not see the devastating implications of his own phrase "Wherever he transports himself he sees only himself." It is true of Thomas, and it means that he cannot escape the bonds of his infantile egocentricity. He seeks always for total attention from the mother, to whom he must be the whole world: "who / shaped my clayfellow . . . / now make the world of me . . ." This mother love which the world must give must be unconditional—which means that none of the exigencies of reality may impinge. The self must be egoistically protected, and the "not-me" denied.

This need for an impossible degree of approval, toleration and special attention from the world mars Thomas's larger gestures at human themes. In *After the Funeral* there is a typical failure to control the powerful flood of passion: the exalted expression, intended to reduce a hostile and indifferent world to awed respect and honour for a dead woman, becomes so excessively insistent as to defeat its object. We are left only, once more, with a sense of this poet's sense of omnipotent egocentricity, as of the monistic infant.

The failure to achieve mature balance appears worst in the attack on others who fail to grieve as much as he does—in the childish insolence against those who "mule praise" with "Windshake of sailshaped ears . . ."

At one point his own extravagance strikes him, and we have the true voice of self-knowledge, for a while:

> *Though this for her is a monstrous image blindly*
> *Magnified out of praise; her death was a still drop;*
> *She would not have me sinking in the holy*
> *Flood of her heart's fame; she would lie dumb and deep*
> *And need no druid of her broken body*

—why not let her lie then? Why try to be her druid if she doesn't need one? The answer is in the self-deceptive word "sinking"—he is not sinking, truly, but "magnifying out of praise"—rising to be the druid and using her for his own aggrandizement:

> *But I, Ann's bard on a raised hearth, call all*
> *The seas to service . . .*

The momentary glimpse of the reality is turned into an excuse to escape from true grief into the pleasurable flood of feeling as "the only one to care"—the child seeking self-assurance that it is still alive in a flood of remorseful protest.

> Storm me forever over her grave until
> The stuffed lung of the fox twitch and cry Love . . .

The stuffed fox, as a child will self-protectingly believe, can come to life, if sufficient clamour is made. The reality of death is escaped from, by incantory magic.

In the "nobler" poems the *hwyl* is indeed a form of childish incantation directed at magically disarming and dissolving the threats of mortal reality. Thus *Do not go gentle into that good night* (*Collected Poems*, p. 116) is an incantory protest against the poet's father's death enacted by the alliteration of protesting "g's" in the repeated injunction. Enacted too by the incantatory switching of repeated lines, as if to charm the dying man back to life. The feeling is indubitably sincere, and the gesture largely successful. But some of the statements are mimic wisdom and sort badly with the urgent sincerity of the feeling: they seem so contrived:

> Though wise men at the end know dark is night
> Because their words had forked no lightning they
> Do not go gentle . . .

Why the knowledge that "their words had forked no lightning" made the wise men who had accepted death ungentle in dying is not clear, and each reader could understand it differently. The images are merely there, histrionically, to bring in the phrase "forked no lightning" to give a Lear-like grandeur to the dirge. Similarly,

> Grave men, near death who see with blinding sight
> Blind eyes could blaze like meteors and be gay
> Rage, rage . . .

perhaps invokes the Miltonic—but what is the effect of "be gay"? It seems to me sensational, rather hysterical sentimentality, though the injunctions have, of course, a desperate quality of exhortation which is moving in itself. But there is still something which too energetically draws attention to the self, and is therefore to be suspected of a pose—even a pose struck to disguise the true feelings. It is appropriate that this poem should be set as a dirge to Thomas himself by Igor Stravinsky, since the attitude struck in it to death is the poet's own self-centred self-ennobling one, erected out of his inability as eternal infant, to accept his own or human mortality.

The failure to "find anything but himself" is most disastrous in Thomas's religious poems. In *Vision and Prayer* (*Collected Poems*, p. 137) we can see the effects of seeking God, who can only be conceived as God the Thomas. This series of easter-wing and lozenge-shaped poems was presumably undertaken because Thomas claims some racial link with George Herbert. The less said about this the better as one would not wish the shade of Herbert to be troubled by the least suggestion that such a comparison is seriously possible, between such humility as that of Herbert's and Thomas's cosmic egotism and sense of omnipotence: they are at opposite moral poles.

In *Vision and Prayer* Thomas excites from his imagination a vision of Christ being born as if He were Thomas, and prays that Christ should return to the womb. The verse has few qualities which distinguish it from prose, and the devices are used by Thomas to disguise from himself what in fact he is really doing—uttering a denial once more of time and the reality of mortal growth mixed with a large measure of neurotic resentment at the birth of other children—especially Christ—than himself. He prays

> *That he who learns now the sun and moon*
> *of his mother's milk may return . . .*
> *And the womb*
> *Yawn to his upcoming.*

The dead are to be left alone, not resurrected and as

> *beating dust be blown*
> *Down to the river . . .*
> *Under the night forever falling . . .*

The penultimate verse seems to say:
"In the name of the fatherless, the unborn, in the name of no one Now or No one to be I pray—may the crimson sun spin a grave grey and the colour of clay stream upon his martyrdom."

It is difficult to follow the drift, except that he seems to wish all competition, in the womb or from the womb, dead, in the name of no one: in this his unconscious attitude to birth is exposed beneath the surface of a religious-seeming poem. Herbert, in such a poem as *The Collar*, renders his progressing self-knowledge—knowledge of his own childishness: "I heard one calling Childe." Thomas simply does not know what he is doing, and what he *is* doing is to ask to be the one all-important child on earth. He identifies himself with Christ who had his mother (a Virgin) entirely to himself. He is guilty of having wished Jesus back in the womb: but the solution is to become Christ:

> *In the name of the damned*
> *I would turn back and run*
> *To the hidden land*
> *But the loud sun [how?]*
> *Christens down*
> *The sky.*

> *I*
> *Am found.*
> *O let him*
> *Scald me and drown*
> *Me in his world's wound.*
> *His lightning answers my*
> *Cry. My voice burns in his hand.*
> *Now I am lost in the blinding*
> *One . . .*

The series is inconsistent, the drives being governed by the poet's inability to place and order his powerful feelings of jealousy and hostility to infants other than himself, especially the Christ Child, whom he jealously wishes to become by intense identification.

Such energetic egocentricity can only exist in a world of its own—Olson is right in this respect, for Dylan Thomas manufactured a poetic language which was by its nature cut off from the exactions of the inherited English language, as he wished to be cut off from the exactions of reality itself.

Thomas's own accounts of his creation are revealing. The following words of Thomas are quoted by Marjorie Adix in *Dylan Thomas, The Legend and the Poet,* from a debate at the University of Utah:

THOMAS   It is impossible to be too clear. You can state bluntly all you know, or put down very clearly what you intend, which may be very narrow and even cruel. But we don't know about anything. Especially people, nobody knows. There are scientific terms, but—why doesn't the water fly out of the ocean when the earth whirls? Because it is a ball of magic. It is impossible to be too clear. I am trying for more clarity now. At first I thought it enough to leave an impression of sound and feeling and let the meaning seep in later, but since I've been giving these broadcasts and reading other men's poetry as well as my own, I find it better to have more meaning at first reading.

GHISELIN   But, on the other hand, isn't it possible to narrow and fix a meaning to the exclusion of richer levels of meaning?

THOMAS   Oh God, isn't an education wonderful!

GHISELIN   I shall be silent from now on.

THOMAS   No, I mean it as a compliment. You say things so well, and I'm ashamed to be flippant and go down the side-alleys . . .

LADY   Do you revise?

THOMAS   No, I work it out a phrase at a time. It is very slow, but when it is once finished, all the revision has been done, and I don't change it.

The account also reveals how Thomas, once he rose to his feet and read to them, exerted the disarming *hwyl*-appeal. Marjorie Adix goes on:

> I can't express how startling the change was in him, from the shy, humble, apologetic, patiently eager man, to this tidal wave of humanity. I was uneasy at first because I felt that in either one position or the other he was only acting, but I could find no trace of insincerity ever. I suppose he knows best. He is lots of people . . .

It is significant that Thomas is evasively flippant in the exchange: then he reveals his essential opportunism in chasing fortuitous ambiguity by ramification of puns, allusions, verbal contrivances. Ghiselin's remark is most telling—touching on the need for a control of words which defines by excluding irrelevance. Thomas returns to "I work out a phrase at a time"—he "works in," by handling from the outside, manipulated expansions of ambiguity, with no controlling impulse towards order, no impulse from within to explore reality by metaphor responsible to this need. The exchange reveals why it matters that Thomas had no critical powers: he could not discipline his attention to *meaning* sufficiently to *allow* live metaphor to come.

Writing on all other writers he is always talking about himself. Here is Wilfrid Owen-Thomas: "The sombre but radiant, selfless, decrying and exalting, infinitely tender, humble, harrowed seer and stater of the Anthem for Doomed Youth and for himself." Except that Dylan Thomas must have realized that he was not that: "selfless," "humble"—and a bitterness reveals itself later in a sneer at Owen's "safe" background.

Here he is presenting what seems to me an urbane and civilized sonnet by Sir Philip Sidney-Thomas: "In those sounds we see, held still in time for us, a whole progress of passion, physical and spiritual, coursing through rage and despair, self-pity, hope, renewed, exultancy, moon-moved dreams, black fear, and blinding bright certainty of final loss." (If that is Sir Philip Sidney, we have few adjectives left for the perhaps wider ranges of *Wuthering Heights* and *King Lear!*)

One may not demand considered critical essays from every poet: what one does demand is a responsible attitude to the writing of poetry and to the language. Dylan Thomas showed neither: he sheltered behind his *hwyl* and encouraged others to be hypnotized by it too. Some of his letters are published, and Vernon Watkins offers him as a "craftsman." But he appears as a craftsman who handles language very much from the outside, and who hardly ever discusses the intractabilities of the meaning—the meaning of life—which the poetry needs to explore and express.

The impression we get is of a floundering over meaning, which is never closely discussed—a tendency to leave too much to chance and "sound," and to seize opportunities as they come by accident. There is insufficient of the artist's sense of lifelong contest with the nature of life, as expressed in Chaucer's: "The lyf so short, the craft so long to lerne." For instance of the poem "If my head hurt a hair's foot," Thomas writes:

> It is not a narrative, not an argument, but a series of conflicting images which move through pity and violence to an unreconciled acceptance of suffering: the mother's and the child's. This poem has been called obscure. I refuse to believe that it is obscurer than pity, violence or suffering. But being a poem, not a lifetime, it is more compressed.
>
> QUITE EARLY ONE MORNING, p. 13.

What this contribution does is to blur: to blur the division between life and poetry (the implication being again, "this piece of my lifetime's experience—my suffering—criticize it if you dare"). It blurs too the necessary distinction between narrative, argument and *image*: Dylan Thomas seems to have misread some critical notes in *New Bearings in English Poetry* by F. R. Leavis on *Gerontion* ("It has neither narrative nor logical continuity . . .") and reproduces this as a garbled justification for his own poem. How can "images" "move through" pity and violence, except by a process of development by poetic argument, in which they are charged with emotional meaning for us, *the readers?* Thomas speaks as if it were the child's and mother's acceptance of suffering that is involved; whereas such a reconciliation can only arrive, exist, by the efforts of construction of the poet, and be realized in the possession of the poem by its readers. He is confusing life and art. Obscurity would be justified if the readers could, by their collective efforts, be brought to experience the acceptance of suffering. But to say "it is not obscurer than pity, violence, or suffering" is begging the question, for by that argument any old nonsense could be justified by the poet's saying, well this is about life, and life's obscure: it is a this-is-a-painting-of-a-black-cat-in-a-dark-cellar argument. In fact anyone may say what they suppose the meaning is, and not only "communication" but the ordering and exploring process itself has broken down.

It is obvious from his own statements on his craft that Dylan Thomas's trouble was largely that he did not know what he was doing:

> I make one image—though 'make' is not the word; I let, perhaps, an image be 'made' emotionally in me and then apply to it what intellectual and critical forces I possess—let it breed another, let that image contradict the first, make, of the third image bred out of the other two together, a fourth contradictory image, and let them all, within my imposed formal limits, conflict.
>
> Quoted by Geoffrey Moore, . . .
> *The Legend and The Poet.*

The impression one gets is of mere opportunism—not of "getting the better of words," but of exploiting chance effects by chance. What one does demand from a poem in its emergence from life is not concoction, but the discipline of sincere and responsible attention to the voices of inner reality, of emotion and thought. But this process must come live, not be forced. The poet must be at "the growing point of consciousness," otherwise he can offer us nothing, not even good entertainment, that we can't provide for ourselves. Can we believe that a poet who can speak of his work on the lines "look at these things! Almost poetry!" is being serious enough to merit our consideration? "Reading one's own poems aloud is letting the cat out of the bag. You may have always suspected bits of a poem to be overweighted, over violent, or daft" (*Reading One's Own Poems*). Yet Thomas was unable to do anything about these faults when he did see them: he himself accepts his poems as bardic ejaculations. In 1950 he wrote of the last of *Three Poems:* "When I have cleared up some of its more obviously overlush, arch and exuberant mauve *gauche* moments . . ." The irresponsible verbalism is characteristic: but in fact the poem as published two years later in *Collected Poems* varies only slightly.

I have tried to deal here with the strongest feature of Dylan Thomas's reputation. Olson is a critic who from sound common sense finds him verbose, strained, obscure, sentimental, apt to excite himself unnecessarily, able to write better than he did, lacking in the outflow of sympathy towards others, and essentially self-centred. But he does not see these as serious objections to the poet's being considered as a significant poet. He remains hypnotized by Thomas's *hwyl*, cowed by Thomas's public acclaim, and disarmed by his appeal. There are many such responses and it has been a matter of approval that Dylan Thomas was conspicuously devoid of critical ability, of his own work as well as that of others, that he shows neither an adequate conception of what poetry is, nor, at any point between the intense solemnity of his birth-and-death poetry and the comic advertisement-copy language of some of his B.B.C. talks, any indication of how seriously he meant his work to be taken. Criticism of Dylan Thomas has always been stupid (as Miss Sitwell proclaimed in *Atlantic*), obtuse, or sacrilegious.

The collection *Dylan Thomas, The Legend and The Poet* contains many examples of critical self-deception. Here, for instance, is Karl Shapiro: these strictures do not matter:

> Even when we examine the texture of his language we fail to find anything original. There are a few tricks of word order, a way of using a sentence, a characteristic vocabulary, an obsessive repetition of phrase, and so on—things common to many lesser poets. Again, if we

analyse his images and metaphors, which are much more impressive than the things I have mentioned, we frequently find over-development, blowsiness and euphemism, on the one hand, and brilliant crystallization on the other. But no system, no poetic, no practice that adds up to anything you can hold on to. The more you examine Thomas as a stylist the less you find . . .

nor this:

Thomas sometimes attempted to keep people from understanding his poems (which are frequently simple, once you know the dodges). He had a horror of simplicity—or what I consider to be a fear of it . . .

nor this, for "forced" optimism is given the benefit of "affirmation":

And, finally, the forced optimism in the last poems such as 'In Country Sleep', in which, although the whole sequence is unfinished, there is a recognizable affirmation of faith in life.

So, the recoil from love does not matter either:

In place of love, about which Thomas is almost always profoundly bitter, there is sex, the instrument and the physical process of love. The activity of sex, Thomas hopes in his poems, will somehow lead to love in life and in the cosmos. As he grows older, love recedes and sex becomes a nightmare, a Black Mass.

A poet like Richard Eberhart, while he sees what is wrong with Thomas, is encouraged by such prevalent valuations to conclude that Thomas's masking of reality is really a means to seek a deeper reality:

The fact is that we live the truth but cannot tell the truth. Poetry is involved in the truth and is the final truth, but, by paradox, it is a parcel of myth; which is to use the word not in peroration but in praise, and to use another word were probably better. Say then poetry is myth or sleight-of-hand-sleight-of-mind tricks to show iridescent qualities of the soul. *Is not Thomas's poetry a continuous artifice in this sense, a series of masks each paradoxically revealing the truth, or part of the truth, and is not his conscious craftsmanship itself an ability of the self to fend off reality* so that reality will not be used up, a deftness to vary the conception with every poem, with every year, with every new insight, a consuming making of reality in the form of poetry, so that the total depth of life will never be exhausted?

My italics are to show the suppressed truth which Eberhart sees. The mask is not, however, to prevent reality being "used up," but to prevent its being engaged in a contest with reality at all. For the rest, Eberhart sees, but does not mind, the disabling sickness:

> I had to (and was delighted to) get him up in the morning by plugging his mouth with a bottle of beer, this wonderful baby.

Some critics do realize the implications for his work of such immaturity—this is a penetrating comment by D. S. Savage:

> One is led, furthermore, to wonder to what extent the too simple celebration of childhood, predominantly descriptive and correspondingly devoid of imaginative-metaphysical insight is permissibly to be termed retrogressive; as indicating, that is, a deliberate avoidance of the complexities (which exist on the active level of moral choice and psychological discrimination) of adult, mature experience.

But what we often have is the kind of process we see in Francis Scarfe's essay. He makes the appropriate observations:

> the rhythms are monotonous enough to make this pall . . . His basic device is the making of words . . .

(Thomas says) 'Poetry is the rhythmic, inevitably narrative, movement from an overclothed blindness to a naked vision', and his definition of his poetic activity as '. . . the physical and mental task of constructing a formally watertight compartment of words, preferably with a main moving column' (*New Verse*, October 1934) . . .

> . . . Unfinishedness is regarded by some as an insult to the reader, but in reality it is honest, and one of the most attractive aspects of his work . . .
> . . . 'man of leaves', 'tree of nettles', 'wood of weathers', 'sixth of wind', 'house of bread'. This is very charming at first, but it *bores by repetition* . . . That his poems still startle our complacency is a proof that *his first appeal was not due to mere bogus verbalism*. It is well that he is losing some of these habits, which lead to *preciousness of the most pompous kind*. Not that it matters . . . [italics supplied]

Thomas's own personality begs, and receives, the allowances such critics as Scarfe make, even when they have perceived his poetry as incompetent, boring, bogus, unfinished. And because of one approving reference Thomas makes to Freud they assume he has the self-knowledge he so patently and disastrously lacks. Self-knowledge in poetry can only go with metaphorical vitality and that discipline which is the discipline of offering finished work in the struggle with words and the soul: "each venture / Is a new beginning, a raid on the inarticulate . . ." The process of writing changes the writer,

> Because one has only learnt to get the better of words
> For the thing one no longer has to say, or the way in which
> One is no longer disposed to say it . . .
>
> T. S. ELIOT, EAST COKER, FOUR QUARTETS.

This process Dylan Thomas never entered into, being too actively engaged in *not* allowing himself to change or grow.

But others let us in to the secret of the intense power of the child-spirit taking over the man, and making the infantile appeal—through incantation and *hwyl*—to disarm the public: "What struck me particularly then was the immense trouble he took over every detail of timing, volume, expression, and the *incantatory gestures he used to work himself up to the right pitch*." (JOHN LEHMANN, *Dylan Thomas, The Legend and the Poet*; [italics supplied.])

To women, of course, he had the child appeal to mother: "he revealed a large and remarkable head, not shaggy—for he was visiting—but heavy with a hair the dull gold of three-penny bits springing in deep waves and curls from a precise middle parting . . . I lost touch with him at the beginning of the war. I only knew him as a boy. He is that to me still . . ." (*Pamela Hansford Johnson, ibid.*)

But Dylan Thomas was also largely protected against adverse criticism by the very nature of his verse itself, a cunning oral defence of its own against reality. Half of it is meaningless, and this explains a good deal of the critical self-deception. The energetic pleas in Thomas's poetry for special consideration for infantile weaknesses of personality touched on everyone's own weaknesses of the same kind: the fear of exposing immaturities of our own makes us prefer to take Thomas's infant solemnity seriously rather than seek to expose it, because in doing so we must expose ourselves. And Thomas was taken seriously, as 454 books and articles listed in Elder Olson's book reveal. But where does he himself indicate that he wishes his poetry to be taken seriously? If the answer is in the poetry, we will try to find it there.

Above all he longed for his mother's breast
Which was rest, and dust . . .

ELEGY.

WHATEVER CLAIMS there may have been made for
Dylan Thomas, it cannot be denied that as Mr. A. T.
Davies says, "(there are) many whose appreciation of
his verse needed the persuasion of the poet's own interpretation," and that this interpretation was largely
a matter of delivery. Though he is said by the same
writer to have "the sensitive and sure discrimination
natural to the poet," there is nothing in the prose
writings of Dylan Thomas to assist our discriminating
response to his poetry. Indeed, wherever he writes
about his work he does so in a remarkably off-hand and
even irresponsible manner. Even in his recordings he
made frequent errors in his own poems, while he
speaks of creation as a kind of word game: "The dear,
daft time I take to nudge the sentence" (*Today This
Insect*). But in examining Dylan Thomas's poems
closely it would seem appropriate perhaps to begin
with one he chose to read on the radio, without
introduction or gloss, as one of his best (*Collected
Poems*, p. 125):

There was a saviour
Rarer than radium,
Commoner than water, crueller than truth;
Children kept from the sun
Assembled at his tongue
To hear the golden note turn in a groove,
Prisoners of wishes locked their eyes
In the jails and studies of his keyless smiles.

The voice of children says
From a lost wilderness
There was calm to be done in his safe unrest,
When hindering man hurt
Man, animal, or bird
We hid our fears in that murdering breath,
Silence, silence to do, when earth grew loud,
In lairs and asylums of the tremendous shout.

There was glory to hear
In the churches of his tears,
Under his downy arm you sighed as he struck,
O you who could not cry
On to the ground as a man died
Put a tear for joy in the unearthly flood
And laid your cheek against a cloud-formed shell:
Now in the dark there is only yourself and myself.

Two proud, blacked brothers cry,
Winter-locked side by side,
To this inhospitable hollow year,
O we who could not stir
One lean sigh when we heard
Greed on man beating near and fire neighbour
But wailed and nested in the sky-blue wall
Now break a giant tear for the little known fall,

For the drooping of homes
That did not nurse our bones,
Brave deaths of only ones but never found,
Now see, alone in us,
Our own true strangers' dust

Ride through the doors of our unentered house.
Exiled in us we arouse the soft,
Unclenched, armless, silk and rough love that
     breaks all rocks.

Our first difficulty is the *possible* meaning of the poem rather than its total meaning—even allowing for a great deal of ambiguity (of the wrong sort) we cannot begin to grasp a poem until we have what Mr. Eliot calls the "bone" for that "housedog," the mind—an idea of what the poem is about.

Perhaps our first step may be to notice that in some places the half-rhymes have been created by manipulations which add nothing but make the sense more difficult to come by—"The voices of children say" or "speak" has been manipulated to provide the "says" "-ness" half-rhyme. The difficulty of "to hear" comes because of the half-accomplished attempt to produce a half-rhyme in the first two lines of stanza three. So we can approach the whole poem's meaning with a sense of its being to a large extent half-finished, and somewhat awkwardly manipulated into shape.

This technical impotence goes with the wider pervading sense of impotence in Dylan Thomas's work, an impotence of language belonging to an impotence in living. "O God, he thought, make me feel something . . . I must be impotent": so thinks Samuel Bennet, that autobiographical character in *Adventures in the Skin Trade*. Characteristically, and as with another autobiographical character in *Portrait of the Artist as a Young Dog*, Samuel Bennet's love-making ends in some form of oblivion induced (by drinking eau-de-cologne) before the hero and the woman can make love in the body.

The impotence in this writer goes with the shrinking from adult life and its exigencies: it penetrates even to his equivocal punctuation. Only in the child-role can he, albeit breathlessly, speak, and this alone produced the few remarkable pieces such as *Fern Hill*. (It also explains the curious emotions of older women in dealing with Dylan Thomas as a poet-person.[1])

But to return to *There was a Saviour*, and the possible meaning. Here is my first effort at elucidation. I do not suppose that a poem can be paraphrased: but here it would seem necessary—indicatively—that the poem should be paraphrased, to show that the verse is but a complicated way of saying something which prose would reveal as inept. The poem is an unsatisfactory way of putting something that is better said in prose if it is worth saying at all: and the complications are not the felt complications in grappling with experience that we have in, say, the poetry of Hopkins:

> There was once a saviour of mankind who was at the same time of a rarer quality than radium, more common than water, and crueller than truth.
>
> Children kept from the sun (that is, sheltered by custom and religious belief and practice from vitality) assembled to hear his words, to hear his golden voice which worked much as a key in a lock, or a gramophone needle, repeating the same old matter and locking up the soul. Those people who were imprisoned by their own dreams of a future life and the Kingdom of Heaven thereby locked up their vision of things in the jails and studies (like the cells of monks) of his smiles, (his gentle good humour?) which had no key to unlock anything. The voice of children crying from a lost wilderness (perhaps the lost wilderness of our own childhood, or the poet's own childhood) says that it was possible to achieve a calm in the safe but restless uncertainty of his promises. When man, who interferes and hinders, hurt man, animal or bird we hid our fears (of this cruelty which is the world's and is part of life) in the saviour's murdering words—murdering because they destroyed our true vitality. There was quiet, quiet in which things

could be done, when the world was noisy, in the secret lairs and asylums of the church, which is but itself a great shout of affirmation.

There was glory to be heard in the churches which told of (or were built of) the tears of Jesus, of his suffering. Under his downy arms (like those of an angel) you sighed (with gratitude or "unrest"?) as he struck you. O you (the poet is addressing himself), who could not cry on earth when man died, you put a tear all the same into the flood of tears belonging to the unearthly flood of them—tears, that is, belonging to the spiritual myth and not the reality of the world. And you comforted yourself by placing your cheek against the shell shaped like a cloud—(that is, you listened as a child does to a sea-shell to hear an imaginary sea?)

Now, in the dark, now we have discovered there is no Saviour, now we have lost our belief, there is only yourself and myself (either the poet and himself, or the poet and the reader, or, at a long shot, the poet and his love, or the poet and his mother—though there follows a reference to "brothers"). Two proud benighted brothers we cry out, locked by the winter of spiritual darkness together, to this year without comfort, to this hollow year. O we who could not produce one lean sigh when we heard men being greedy to one another, beating one another, near and far neighbours, in fire, but wailed and shrank into visions of a life behind the sky, into visions which protected us, now we cry hugely because the Saviour is gone, there has been another fall of man, and few people know of it, and because of the war's catastrophe, houses destroyed or damaged which were not our homes, because of the brave deaths of lonely people never found (? under the debris) now see, we have found in ourselves, our own true clay which makes us strange one from another but which is our true self. This clay or dust rides through the doors of a new house which has never yet been entered. Cast out so that we have to rely upon ourselves, not on a saviour, we arouse the soft, unclenched, unarmed, silk and rough love that breaks all rocks—is more enduring than reality.

The poem is thus an attempt to say a number of things to do with attitudes to experience: it is perhaps the poem in which Dylan Thomas came nearest to the attempt to organize deeply felt experience, and yet it is probably his most meaningless poem. The different elements are these:

The rejection of religious faith as delusive and destructive of vitality.

The loss of faith, which brings mourning for the loss of the saviour and the catastrophe of war (?how):

But which loss of deceptive faith leaves "us" alone to find a triumph in our love as "true" dust.

The latter, it would seem, not being the love between the poet and a woman, because he specifically refers to "brothers," which must either be between him and himself, or between him and the reader ("*mon semblable, mon frère*").

Having thus written out at length what I take to be the paraphrasable meaning of the poem, I expect to find, turning back to the poem, that I have produced a crudified version (as I feel I would have done if, say, I attempted to paraphrase Donne's *Exstasie* or Blake's *Sick Rose*). Yet, turning back to the poem I can only see it as an inadequate and incomplete attempt to render what I take to be the intended meaning.

In many places I have had to do work—to interpret and interpolate by guesswork—which as a reader I should not have had to do. The meaning should be *there* if I take sufficient care as a reader. Rhythm and movement in poetry should help enact a meaning that is only damaged by paraphrase. Here I do not find them adding to what I take to be the intended meaning. Nor do the qualities of the texture of the verse help create attitudes to the experience rendered.

What seems to be complexity is often merely irresponsibility or laziness in leaving a half-finished figure—often it is a deliberate perversity. The first perversity is in the irresponsibility about punctuation: commas are used at the ends of lines 6, 11, 14, 18, 19, 27, 35 when, to help the reader and to assist the poem's structure, a colon, semi-colon or full-stop should have been used. To be deliberately vague about punctuation in this way produces perplexity in the reader and is intended to stand instead of genuine complexity and involvement. In serving the purpose only of making the poem seem more difficult it is an affectation: a related affectation—making for unnecessary difficulty —is Dylan Thomas's omission of hyphens in hyphenated pairs of words.

Neither should the poet be clumsy about syntax: "Two proud, blacked brothers cry." "Blacked" means *coloured black by the act of blacking*: it implies something blacking something, for *to black* is a transitive verb. To *black out* can be intransitive, and *blackened* is the adjectival past participle from *to blacken*, and feels more intransitive. Boots are *blacked*, and we talk of a *boot-black*. And we talk of *black men*, and *black brothers*.

To a poet (if a poet is in the van of our use of language to explore experience) such auras of a common word would have been unconsciously present, at the tip of the mind's fingers. They are patently not so to Dylan Thomas.

Dylan Thomas was careful to avoid *blackened* (which has a pejorative flavour) and *black* (which would have suggested the brothers were negroes), but he has forgotten boots and coons. The activity of the word *blacked*, if one is sensitive to the English language, does not evoke darkness, spiritual or otherwise. The poet may, of course, have wanted to suggest the blackout (see below), and *blacked-out* would then have been preferable to *blacked*. *Blacked*, too, has an inappropriate everyday sound, as compared, say, with *darkness*, which is more mysterious in flavour. The activity of the word *blacked*, if one is responding normally to English, is not that of suggesting *benighted* or *darkened*, and is all extraneous flavour here, an irrelevant activity as of applying a soft black pigment.

Even Vernon Watkins took this word up with Thomas, but all the poet did was to justify the external sound-effect of the word: "I like the word 'blacked' by the way in spite of its, in the context, jarring dissonance with 'locked.' I had, quite apart (that is absurd, I mean secondarily to) from the poem, the blackout in mind, another little hindrance on the scene, and the word seemed to me to come rightly."

Everything is left to chance and sound—in the Sitwellian way—and language is handled for effect from the outside, not from the deep inward intractable voice of true metaphor. That is one kind of syntactical, verbal irresponsibility. A more general weakness in the same stanza is this:

> O we who could not stir
> One lean sigh when we heard
> Greed on man beating near and fire neighbour.

"Stir," given emphasis by the line-break, puzzles for a moment, and in any case has no great felicity as "stir . . . a sigh": perhaps it was manufactured from "stir a limb" and Dylan Thomas may have been recalling Hopkins's "spare a sigh" in *Spring and Fall*. But the syntax of the rest of the phrase has been deliberately manipulated to increase "ambiguity," so that it becomes meaningless in the ordinary sense of the word.

> *We could not sigh when we heard greed on man*
> *beating near and fire neighbour.*

Now one can grasp a general meaning: "we could not sigh *though* we heard greed *in* man causing him to beat his near and far neighbour *with fire*." That is, when we heard war's catastrophes, fire raids caused by man's greed, and causing him to beat his neighbour.

But, again, one's paraphrases seem so much to be preferred to the line of poetry. There the odd prepositions ("*on* man") seem deliberately obstructive and perverse. The verb itself, "beating" seems on the whole weak. "*When* we heard" suggests the event happening once and once only (unlike "whenever"). And the "near and *fire*" seems merely a distractive trick, for "fire" becomes substituted for "far," and the "far neighbour" becomes a "fire neighbour," though one might have expected both the near and far neighbour to suffer from fire. The change from "far" to "fire" is an attempt at the kind of thing Hopkins achieves (also in *Spring and Fall*) in "ghost guessed": but such movements of one word into another must go with a movement of the verse, and a movement of meaning, a poetic logic. This poetry has less poetic logic than the prose paraphrase one can make of it.

For the logic of the poem, however one reads it, is nonexistent. Indeed, one might say that the tricks of manipulation serve only to give an apparent significance to a miserably thin statement, and to a poem which is without felt structure whether emotional, of mood, or of "intellectual" adherence.

> *Once we believed in Jesus: that was a delusion.*
> *Now we are without faith.*

*When we had faith we had no sympathy for other's
    suffering.
Now we mourn the loss of Jesus, and the catastrophes
    of war.
Now see our love triumphing.*

The pattern is incomplete, in that the love is not
triumphant in producing either the undeluded awareness of life, or the sympathy the brothers could not
extend when they were deluded by the Saviour. What
the war has to do with the matter is not at all clear,
except that it is happening. Nor is the quality of the
love expressed in anything other than by an evocation
of its tactile quality and the vague "break all rocks":
there is no "doing" in the poetry, no feel in the mouth
of texture in the verse, as there is, for instance even in
folk-song such as "Until the seas run dry my love/
The rocks melt in the sun." The unrelieved platitudes
of "soft," "unclenched," "silk and rough" remain
cliché, while "armless" seems to me fatuously inappro-
pirate.[2] These are verbal gestures "worked up" in cold
blood. It cannot, except by a violence to the language,
be taken to mean "unarmed," while love, essentially,
we feel to have its strength conventionally, in the arms
of embrace. An "armless" love suggests perhaps even
something morbid or even perverted. The line may be
a wild gesture at the ecstasies of the child-mother
relationship—"unclenched" and "armless" evoking the
absence of the claims and exigencies of adult love. But
the words are wild.[3]

There is the same inappropriateness about "the
drooping of homes," if words are to have any common
meaning at all to which poetry shall add intensity.
Houses can fall, crumble, decay, disintegrate; homes
which one feels as connected with "houses" can be
broken up or deracinated, and no doubt poetry can
refurbish these commonplaces. But how can a home

"droop"? The texture suggested by that combination of words remains to me utterly unconvincing, and indeed ludicrous, merely playful.

So throughout the poem, the imagery is for the most part unrealizable—one cannot, that is, allow it to form either as something seen, or grasped, or felt in the limbs or mouth-movement. "Radium" is something of which we have only intellectual knowledge, that water is common is a truism, and that truth is cruel is a platitude. Children kept from the sun—the "kept from" is a negative and bodiless phrase to convey devitalization. Compare "keep" which suggests in Hopkins's *Golden Echo* by its mouth movement, a kind of cupboard-closing, positive and desired muscular action.

> How to keep
> *Back beauty.*

"Assembled," "tongue," "golden note," "groove," "locked" suggest a mechanical agglomeration of locks and gramophones which I can fit into no organized order of metaphorical pattern. And if you can have a "keyless smile" (presumably derived from the wartime coinage "clueless"), what does a smile which *has* a key or keys look like? (As Hopkins pointed out to Bridges, a "–less" word suggests the thing which-it-is-less as in Bridges's line: "High in the domeless courts of proud Olympus," where one sees, inevitably, domes where none should be).

But there is no need to go on in such detail. Without either concision of meaning or order of structure the poem can have no emotional unity either. The rhythm of affirmation at the end is childishly breathless, and the rhythm of the poem for the main part is that of Beeching's *God Who Created Me* ("nimble and light of limb") and it is very possible that Dylan Thomas was subconsciously echoing that school-taught horror. Certainly the poet makes more use of the power of words endowed with religious (or religiose) flavour than his rejection of the Saviour would seem to warrant. "Keyless" in the first stanza has little critical force as set against "rarer than radium" etc., and "golden": so "safe unrest" suggests a feeling about the belief in the Saviour which makes that "murdering" so sudden and surprising: a good deal of the excitement in the poem is in its unconscious blasphemy and its religiose overtones, and there is a powerful sense in it of a boy thinking wicked thoughts at school assembly (from which perhaps the odd word "assembled" comes).

The final phrase which I want to deal with, as showing the metaphorical weakness, the deadness of language handled from the outside, is: "There was glory to hear,/ In the churches of his tears," meaning "It was glorious to hear the tear-jerking services in the churches in which we worshipped that sorrowful Saviour"—or "there was a glory in His pity which had become the church." What one substitutes varies each time, and this reveals that the poetry has no real economy or precision. Yet this kind of carelessness, about verbs (why change "to be heard" to "to hear"?) and prepositions ("churches of his tears") is taken widely nowadays to be the mark of poetic inspiration. The faculty for realization in poetry—yielding forms of texture and rhythm which enact meaning—is essentially a moral faculty, because it is a habit of exploring experience by metaphor and thus "placing" it. This is the life of language; but the language of *There was a Saviour* has no life: it is dead language so worked on as to convince us that it is remarkable poetry. The working process disguises whatever meaning was sought in the first place, which was not much. Yet this babel-babble has convinced many, and as a curiosity such meaningless concocted poetry will always be of interest, if only as an exhibit in a strange case-history. It is words "assembled" in opportunist ways—the poet adds this to that, and then something else is worked in, and sees, yes, he can add that. By such means poetry is nowadays widely manufactured, in the place of the real thing which can only come from the drives of the true metaphorical impulse, rooted in our need to explore inner reality.

There was a Saviour seems to me to all intents and purposes meaningless. I find 42 of the 90 poems in Dylan Thomas's *Collected Poems* meaningless, or yielding no meaning worth possessing even with the most considerable effort.

Of the following poems I can make nothing at all: p. 6, *A process in the weather of the heart*; p. 24, *Light breaks where no sun shines* (vague images of sex—"a candle in the thighs," "showing its hairs": but mainly nonsense); p. 30, *My world is pyramid*; p. 44, *Shall gods be said to thump the clouds*; p. 46, *Do you not father me*; p. 50, *Was there a time*; p. 51, *Now* (factitious nonsense concealing some aspect of his sexual life: "the come-a-cropper rider of the flower"); p. 56, *How soon the servant sun*; p. 77, *Because the pleasure bird whistles*; p. 91, *How shall my animal*; p. 93, *The tombstone told me when she died*; p. 95, *A Saint about to fall*; p. 107, *To others than you*; p. 108, *Love in the asylum*; p. 117, *Deaths and Entrances*. No doubt some of these might prove illuminating as providing help in analysing Thomas's case-history, but they are so incoherent on the whole that there could be little agreement on what meaning there is in them. Of course this is a gift for the academic critic.

Here we touch on the next strange aspect of Dylan Thomas's popularity: his poetry sold widely and he is everywhere a known image. He wrote some excellent short stories, it is true, and *Under Milk Wood* has had a certain success, which is not only *succès de scandale*. But the fact is that he is most widely known as a poet—yet his poetry is mostly so meaningless that it cannot in fact, really, have been read. How has this happened?

Here once more we must walk on the brink of the limits of literary criticism—and this predicament is forced on us by the nature of the case. Dylan Thomas sought to disguise from himself, as many of us do, suffering from greater or lesser psychic disability, the nature of adult reality. Unconsciously he desired to return to the blissful state of "perfect" experience at the mother's breast. But he had poetic gifts, and it is the nature of poetry to seek reality through metaphor. This, as his few true poems reveal, he could not bear, because it would mean relinquishing the delusions of infant hallucination in favour of painful reality. Because of the nature of his world—our twentieth-century literary society—its immaturity, and its tendency towards such evasions, he was able to find acceptance and popularity *because* of his very immaturity. He invented a babble-language which concealed the nature of reality from himself and his readers—and in its very oral sensationalism, in its very meaninglessness, it represented for him and his readers a satisfying return to the delusions of that stage of infancy when we tend to resist the uncomfortable exigencies and losses consequent upon the development of a growing reality sense. This may be linked with the man's alcoholism and his sexual promiscuity. But besides the appeal in the personality, the poetry as baby-prattle has a tremendous disarming effect of its own—the effect of involving all our weaknesses in a special plea for his. You don't smack a baby: and so every attitude to Dylan Thomas accepts the dangerous amorality of the engaging *enfant terrible*.

Once one detects the nature of the pressure—symbolized perhaps by Richard Erberhart's revelation that Dylan Thomas ("that wonderful baby") needed to be woken up at times by inserting a bottle of beer in his mouth—many aspects of this poet's work and appeal fall into place. His opportunist manipulation of language "from the outside," for instance—"I add this to that, and then, yes I can turn this round to make a pun, good . . ."—this becomes an activity pressed on him by the need to "make a mask"—to perpetuate a deception and a disguise, sometimes by the anaesthesia of *hwyl*, sometimes by sensationalism, sometimes by sheer incoherence.

Much of the poetry may be like raw material for psychoanalysis, as Karl Shapiro has noted: but it is without the development imposed on such raw material by the analytical disciplines of intelligence, by the clinical experience of the psychotherapist: much of it indeed is like the mock-material an analytical patient seems to manufacture to put the analyst off the true scent. And, because it is manipulated for the purposes of disguise, much of it has no roots in the true ordering centres of the imagination—because access to those is blocked and thwarted by fear.

This blockage of the poetic processes in a sensitive and gifted man was not only the consequence of his own psychic weaknesses. It was also a consequence of the way he was taken up for those very weaknesses of his personality, and encouraged to develop the very traits which destroyed him and his talents. This is the strangest feature of Dylan Thomas's notoriety—not that he is bogus, but that attitudes to poetry attached themselves to him which not only threaten the prestige, effectiveness and accessibility of English poetry, but also destroyed his true voice and, at last, him.

One does not have to look far to find further

confirmation of my diagnosis in the poems themselves. In the first few poems in *Collected Poems* we find that this wild voice is mimicking the infant's attention-demanding prattle. It is obvious too that this has both sexual motives, and relates to the anxiety at the loss of the "paradise" of the time of suckling. *I see the boys of summer* (p. 1) is a muddle of extravagant sexual imagery from "tide" for the female sexual organ to "pouch" and "cargoed apple" for scrotum and testicles, to "poles" for the phallus. Were it not for the hints of sexual meaning ("here love's damp muscle dries") few surely, would give such incoherence a second look? Yet it has the power it is meant to have, to compel our attention on infantile exhibitionism — compare Thomas's poem *Once below a time* which renders his infant sexual exhibitionism ("With my cherry capped dangler") in childish ways. The point of such exhibitionism is to make an oral-verbal claim on the mother — the poet wants to possess his mother, and the babble-poetry is the attempt to do this. Time, and the father, are death, because they remove the child from the bliss of innocence and usurp his place with the mother. In *When once the twilight locks no longer* Thomas displays a neurotic horror of death, in relation to the lost joys of suckling:

> The mouth of time sucked, like a sponge,
> The milky acid . . .
> And swallowed dry the waters of the breast . . .
> And mother milk was stiff as sand . . .

Growing up ("I sent my creature scouting on the globe") brings the approaching awareness of mortal reality, which, because he cannot bear it, the poet describes in repulsive hysterical imagery: "Some dead undid their bushy jaws/ And bags of blood let out their flies . . ." Significantly, "bush" and "undid," make this sexual, too, as does "flies," and these allusions show that the horror is a horror of adult sexual reality as well as death. But this true content of the poem is concealed in a banter of mock-verse and extravagant language: the capacity to order is not there, and meaning breaks down, so that reality as a whole can be avoided, and not seen. Similar poems about his fear of sexual reality as an aspect of reality, expressing recoil, are *Where once the waters of your face* (p. 11) and *If I were tickled by the rub of love* (p. 11).

The relation between Thomas's "apocalyptic" vision and the search for personal reality is obvious in *I fellowed sleep* (p. 26). This is apocalyptic dream, and can be followed through a vague process, and personal poignant images may even be grasped: "My father's ghost is climbing in the rain." But the poem is too personal, too much like a patient's dream-for-a-psychoanalyst, to convey any general meaning. The apocalyptic vision symbolizes no common predicament except perhaps the common fantasy of seeking contact with the dead. Significantly Thomas associates his separation fear with the need to "gab" to find his parent contact—each "grave gabbing shade," "Raised up a voice and, climbing on the words."

The dream is, I suppose, an Oedipus dream: he is talking to his mother's ghost, which cries "This that we tread was, too, your father's land." The father, ousted, is "An old, mad man still climbing in his ghost." But the psychic meaning of this dream cannot have been accepted by Thomas—it is disguised by many wild phrases ("Each sung a love," "The inches monkeyed"), and by us must be regarded as meaningless. We have the sense of listening in to a psychoanalytic patient "associating" freely—and there is no one to tell the patient how he is disguising his more painful meanings from himself and us.

The nature of the personal mythology becomes

more apparent in the famous *Altarwise by owl-light* (p. 71), a series of sonnets. They contain violent imagery of sexual injury, mixed with "apocalyptic vision" and Biblical imagery—references to Christ's birth mixed with the poet's birth, and Eve's copulation with the serpent mixed with the child-poet's loss of innocence. There is an occasional disgusting image of recoil from life:

> *The bagpipe breasted ladies in the deadweed*
> *Blew out the blood gauze through the wound of*
> *manwax . . .*

and the poems become pretentious nonsense, lacking in true rhythm and metaphorically inert. If there is anything to be found it is the posturing as of a child convinced of his importance—exhibiting his genital organ ("my long gentleman") and asserting he is as important as Christ: the only reaction in an adult, to an adult behaving in such ways, is boredom at the insistence, however much we may feel pity for the need of a soul to offer such a babble of infantile claim—"old cock from nowheres . . ."—instead of the true voice of poetry.

Later in the poems there is a conflict between the poet's self-exploring honesty about his sexual difficulties in adult relationship, and his attempt to disguise these difficulties from himself and us. Such conflict appears in *I make this in a warring absence* (p. 78).

We can make little of this except that the poet has quarrelled with his love, goes off to sulk and is full of hate of her, cools down and goes back for forgiveness. The process is not delineated in such a way as can be followed in our nerves and senses—there is no felt rhythm. The account of love is extravagant:

> *Whalebed and bulldance, the gold bush of lions,*
> *Proud as a sucked stone, and huge as sandgrains . . .*

—but the account of sexual love dissolves into nonsense. The behaviour and the feeling seem strangely
infantile, and valued as that rather than placed as
such. Thomas characteristically wants love to be of the
cosmic kind he had with the mother. The child-
spirit wants "milk mansion" and the tremendous
nonsensical babble-satisfactions of a relationship with
Mummy. If he can't have this, he will kill Mummy, or
die to spite her (though he is speaking of his adult
woman mate)—here are the springs of Thomas's oral
sadism:

> *Storm her sped heart . . .*

> *And, for that murder's sake, dark with contagion*
> *Like an approaching wave I sprawl to ruin . . .*

Such total possession by hate is only encountered in
the child or dissociated adult. At last he returns to the
mother's forgiving breast: when he is given what he
demanded in infantile anger, he will give his love:

> *Now in the cloud's big breast lie quiet countries . . .*

> *And though my love pulls the pale, nippled air,*
> *Prides of tomorrow suckling in her eyes,*
> *Yet this I make in a forgiving presence.*

Seeking out such meaning is what a study of the
poet's psychopathology might undertake. To consider
this worth making would be to assume Thomas more
than one interesting case out of a thousand, and this
again is to assume that Thomas is of first importance
as a poet. But how can he be so, when the inner reality
such as he expresses here is one by which it would be
impossible to live—since it makes love so conditional,
as a baby tries to before it has begun to learn to love?
Yet Thomas endorses this concept of love and seeks to
persuade us, by his air of "nobility," to share it. In this
he seeks to charm us away from the real and adult.

With such confusion in the private poetry, it is little wonder that the "public" subjects are handled with small success. *Ceremony After a Fire Raid* (p. 129), for instance, is an accumulation of fragments from the liturgy, from Eliot's *Ash Wednesday*, put together to make a dirge about a child killed in an air raid. The elegy is unfortunately mostly incomprehensible— though it evokes many stock religious responses— but it falls short of coherence because it becomes childish incantation against death rather than a compassionate approach to its reality. The poem culminates in the tremendous-sounding, reverberating, but really somewhat meaningless line: "The sundering ultimate kingdom of genesis' thunder . . ." The repeated "und" sounds enact a sense the end belonging to the beginning, and enact the sound of thunder, too, of the end of the world, inherent in the beginning: but the line is still meaningless, for this is not the end of the world; the "kingdom of genesis' thunder" is presumably the world created by the thunder of creation, which cannot be "ultimate" nor is it really "sundering" though it could, I suppose, be "ultimately sundering." Here is poetry used to false ends—made to sound sense when it is in fact merely elevated hollow words, carelessly used, drawing attention more to the "noble" ejaculator of the "ceremony" than to the suffering of victims.

In such poems the impulse seems genuine. In others, such as *When I Wake* (p. 134), it is as if the poet had his hand so well in, in the manufacture of repro poetry, that he began to sacrifice his power of being able ever to write again in a true voice. Other kinds of satisfactions have taken the place of the deepening self-awareness of the true poet.

Cultivating these falsenesses, Thomas progressively cuts himself away from his true voice. At the end *Lie still, sleep becalmed* (p. 136) suffers from the very debility of Thomas's language established by his worst poems: "wound" is used so much elsewhere, so vaguely, that when he wants to use it to *mean* wound (as with the boy who cried "Wolf!" too often for a joke) we cannot respond. This poem has the movement of the true voice: but what "the end of my wound" is we cannot tell, and whether there is a sufferer, or the sea is the sufferer, or why the wound is "the mouth in the throat," [4] or what "ride with you through the drowned" means we cannot tell. The poem therefore fails when it might have been very powerful, and the sorrow and anguish beating at the door of expression are pitifully imprisoned. This—a prevalent meaninglessness—is the inevitable fate of the verbal artist's failure to accept responsibility to language: in the end it is order in life itself which suffers, and causes disordered suffering in the psyche which cannot put behind itself the limitations of infant modes, in favour of a developing, if painful, adult sense of reality. In the end, the arrested child spirit drags the temple of the whole being down on itself. The life ends in a chaos as meaningless as half its poetry.

The lovely gift of the gab bangs back on a blind shaft.

FOR MANY, Dylan Thomas's irresponsibility about his work seemed a cry for liberation. His romanticism is applauded together with both his irresponsible attitude to the task of writing, and to the use of language: they were both part of the appeal—a formidable appeal—to those exasperated by the discipline of Eliot's concern "to purify the dialect of the tribe."

Dylan Thomas's attitude to his work at times was a struck pose of carelessness, and frenzied spontaneity, at least in public: "He wrote upon the block of paper, not knowing what he wrote, and dreading the words that looked up at him at last and could not be forgotten" (A *Prospect of the Sea*, p. 73). Other things he said were: "Where there's a will and a slight delirium there's a way . . . Some of them may be poems . . . Many of them are very odd indeed . . . When in doubt bewilder the b— —s." Whatever allowances we make for the slackness of tone deliberately indulged in at times for success as with a radio audience, it must still seem to us suspicious that a poet should court applause for irresponsibility, for casual disparagement of the artistic conscience, even disguised as modesty. Only if the artist is assured of the worth of his wrestle with experience can we uphold the value of art to life—even discounting the need for an audience ("if I could but get on, if I could but produce work, I should not mind its being buried, silenced, and going no further," G. M. Hopkins wrote to Robert Bridges). But an attitude in which the poet pretends naively to share the shock of the audience at the oddity of his work seems to me to conceal a fundamental desire to compromise with an audience that shrinks from the real disturbances in art—not unconnected with a tendency to bamboozle and to get away with the gesture, for kudos and success. Indeed this is another aspect of Thomas's attempt to disarm criticism, because he must have unconditional approval and approval must include popular acclaim.

Thus, while we may not condemn Dylan Thomas for his grave psychic disabilities, we must for the sake of poetry, because he was a poet, distinguish his weaknesses in composition. A further major disability is his rhythmical failure, which I shall try to relate to his resistances to maturity and reality, also. Here the question of nostalgia enters into the discussion—and aspects of the metaphorical and rhythmical failure can be seen, as I have suggested, to relate to Thomas's yearning for impossibly infantile relationships with people and the world.

The consequence of these weaknesses is the 42 meaningless poems. There are another 40 or so poems which I would call "near poems"—whose meaning collapses in some way at some point or other. Some of these I propose to examine later in this chapter. But first I want to consider rhythm.

Take any one of Dylan Thomas's poems, and it seems a romantic achievement of affirmation: its rhythm seems to elevate. Read through his work, and the poems become a row of romantic affirmations all

looking remarkably similar, and essentially elevated
only, *hwyl*-wise, by factitious rhythms. The result is
tedium. The more one reads through Dylan Thomas's
poetry the more one comes to discover the absence of
anything one can call accomplished craftsmanship, the
craftsmanship which alone can preserve the living
spontaneous rhythm.

Thomas's earlier poems are constructed upon a
stock five-beat line, much less flexible in fact than
Elizabethan blank verse, and without the heroic regular cadence of Marlowe's earlier lines.[1] This five-beat
line will be found to be the basis of most contemporary
vers-libre (much of it is rather *vers-fixe*), by poets who
have never considered, apparently, how completely
un-free, how completely in control, the new and
"freer" forms created by Mr. Eliot are, in *his* hands.

Here is the kind of line I am referring to in Dylan
Thomas:

> *And drown the cargoed apples in their tides* . . .
> *O see the poles are kissing as they cross* . . .
> *The cataracted eyes that filmed their cloth* . . .
> *A process in the weather of the heart* . . .
> *The force that through the green fuse drives the*
>   *flower* . . .
> *If I were tickled by the rub of love* . . .
> *And all the deadly virtues plague my death* . . .

At times this five-beat line, which is the rhythmic
basis of his verse, is modified, for instance by adding a
word, in the simple but striking manner derived from
the opening lines of *The Waste Land*, "I dreamed my
genesis in sweat of sleep, breaking . . ." Sometimes
there is a prefatory broken line, or series of broken
lines:

> *Now*
> *Say nay*

Man dry man
Dry lover mine
The deadrock base and blow the flowered anchor

—but we inevitably find somewhere the "deadrock base" of this five-beat line, to which the poet hangs desperately as a drowning man to a piece of flotsam. And its rhythmic level deadness remains constant: seldom does the texture and impulse of the language override the regular beat. Of the 89 poems and groups of poems in *Collected Poems* only 22 do not at some time or other come to rest on the simple five-beat rhythmic structure.

In a late poem like *In Country Sleep* there are lines of all lengths with very little reason for the variation except for what seems to be a desperate, impotent, effort to escape rhythmic boredom. The poem begins with four five-beat lines, interrupted as it were by a *coda*, "My dear, my dear," followed by two lines, one of six (rather indecipherable) beats, and the last of five. Something of this structure is maintained, but in a very loose fashion, so that the beats in the lines in subsequent stanzas run to an irregular sequence but with no rhythmical interest running close to the meaning.

The basis is the five-beat line, varied merely by careless departures into seven, four, or six beats—not because the meaning insists, but from mere lack of interest. Within the five-beat line it is possible for a poet to achieve amazing extensions or shortenings of length, modulations such as we have in Words-worth's *Sonnet Composed Upon Westminster Bridge*. Consider, for instance, "This city now doth like a garment wear . . ." which is regular, followed by "The beauty of the morning . . ." where the speed and trip of the metre, suggest the eye running over the whole scene. This is followed by the long rhythmical

process of careful and detailed observation in wonder—

> ; *silent, bare*
> *Ships, bowers, domes, theatres, and temples lie*
> *Open* . . .

Here we hear the true voice of poetry, or, if you like,
inspiration. The wonder of the City lying "bare,"
"open" in the "smokeless" air is enacted by the slow
turning metre of the marvelling observation. The "o"
of "open" is the open mouth of wonderment; the
difference between the rhythm of each of these lines is
like the differences between the patterns of one leaf
and another; variations which are organic, alive. The
rhythm in Wordsworth's *Sonnet* enacts the physical
movement of surprise, joy, and the gazing-about at a
panorama. *The poetry does what it says.*

Let me take for comparison the stanza of Dylan
Thomas's which has most variation, and examine the
nature of his departures from his metrical pattern—a
stanza that has beats in each line in the following
pattern: $6/5/5/6$ coda $/5/6/$, stanza 7:

> *(may you)*
> *Lie in grace. Sleep spelled at rest in the lowly house*
> *In the squirrel nimble grove, under linen and thatch*
> *And star: held and blessed, though you scour the high four*
> *Winds, from the dousing shade and the roarer at the latch,*
>
> *Cool in your vows.*
> *Yet out of the beaked, web dark and the pouncing boughs*
> *Be you sure the Thief will seek a way sly and sure*
> *As sly as snow and meek as dew blown to the thorn,*
> *This night and each vast night until the stern bell*
> *talks* . . .

The rhythmical failure, in its lifelessness, belongs to
the failure of meaning.

The poem is to his girl, warning her, in her country
sleep, to fear not the wolf or the tusked prince, but the

Thief ("who falls on the dead like the willy nilly dew") who comes to his love, not to ravish her (note, tide raking wound equals the female sexual organ),

>   *to steal not her tide raking*
> *Wound, not her riding high, nor her eyes, nor kindled hair,*
> *But her faith*

The poem has something of a strict rhyme-scheme, and follows the rough rhythmic pattern, as outlined above, based on a five-beat line varied haphazardly. The rhythm of the piece modulates little, except that it becomes rather more broken and histrionic at the beginning of the second section, where we have the echo of Hopkins, to invoke something of Hopkins's devotional atmosphere:

> *And high, there, on the hare*
> *Heeled winds the rooks . . .*

The country cottage is associated with a natural world given a somewhat antique religious flavour:

> *nunneries and domes of leaves . . .*
>   *three Marys in the rays.*
> *Sanctum, sanctorum the animal eye of the wood*
> *In the rain telling its beads . . .*
>   *Fox and holt kneel before blood . . .*
>   *the Lord's table of the burning grass . . .*
>   *the prayer wheeling moon . . .*

This is associated with the supernatural evil of "hearthstone tales," of the wolf in sheep's clothing, the "broomed witched spume," the "mystic shade or spell"—this the poet says she need not fear, for only moonlight skulks in the dell, and the divine presences as above will protect her: "The country is holy." But the Thief will find a way, as surely as "This night and each vast night" (an echo of the *Lyke-Wake Dirge*) "until the stern bell . . . talks . . . of . . . my own lost love— . . . and the soul walks the waters shorn." The Thief whom the magical incantation is intended to keep away is either Time or Death, because he comes as the "rain falls," "as the dew falls," "as the star falls," or "the winged Apple seed glides, And falls, and flowers in the yawning wound at our sides." Though there is little poetic conciseness in the realization of the Thief, one feels the deficiency in realization comes from a lack of willingness to recognize what the Thief is: at times, indeed, the Thief seems to be something very like maturity, and not at all as predatory as he is made out to be (if he were Time or Death).

After a great deal of excited alarm and preparation, he comes, while the divine creation sings a

> *Music of elements, that a miracle makes!*
>   *All tell, this night, of him . . .*
> *He comes to my love like the designed snow . . .*

(Note how the effect of slow concoction in the word "designed" gives us anything but a live figure which conveys the intended image of snow-flake pattern "designed" by God.)

> *He comes to take*
> *Her faith that this last night for his unsacred sake*
> *He comes to leave her in the lawless sun awaking*
> *Naked and forsaken to grieve he will not come . . .*

The Thief, characteristically, doesn't really come at all. The poet, however, ends by assuring her, in breathless incantation,

> *My dear this night he comes and night without end my*
>   *dear*
> *Since you were born:*
> *And you shall wake, from country sleep, this dawn and*
>   *each first dawn,*
> *Your faith as deathless as the outcry of the ruled sun.*

The poem leaves one, as so many of Dylan Thomas's poems do, with a feeling of unrealization and impotence—which the emphatic oral excitement of the last four lines does nothing to remove. Nothing comes. The diffuse shambling rhythm is the rhythm of nothing being said. Everything seemed set for a development: the contrasting childhood fears and natural divinity presented in excited and striking terms: then the sinister invocation of the Thief who inevitably would "find a way"—here, we might suppose, enters the irony of the adult mature mind about reality. But it is the latter which Dylan Thomas cannot sustain: the Thief becomes life itself: "And surely he sails like the ship shape clouds."

All he manages to take is her "faith," which is even so to remain deathless. What the Thief *is,* is ungraspable, unrealized: he provides merely a vague threat against which to urge all manner of defensive denials, and the final assurance, equally unrealized (faith in what? one asks) is unconvincing under the *hwyl.* The failure in realization is an index of an impotence. It reminds one of a small child's assurance to his mother that he will "protect" her. There is a good deal of verbal sexuality in the poem: "the rind and mire" of love, although a reminiscence of Yeats's "mire and blood," is an indication of the recoil: "tide raking wound" and "riding high" indicate the sometimes desperate sensuality we find in Dylan Thomas's poetry, the desperate sensuality of someone with numbed rather than acute senses: "O God, make me feel something." But here he seeks to wish his girl by incantation into the sexless unreality of a fairy tale, "in the land of the hearth stone tales"—to be the infant-mother controlled by his paranoia and love-demands.

What I find unsatisfactory in the poem I find unsatisfactory in the rhythm of the stanza quoted.

Without demanding any simple contrast between the girl asleep in the cottage and the strange outside natural world, one is, I think, confused by the lack of textural contrast (expressive of attitude towards) between the lines evoking the wild nature, the Thief, and the girl in her country sleep.

> *Lie in grace. Sleep-spelled at rest in the lowly house*
> *In the squirrel-nimble grove, under linen and thatch*

has appropriate labial alliteration, and is quite straightforward Georgian poetry if one inserts the hyphens as the poet should have done: it is reminiscent of the *Innisfree* manner, with a touch of *Away in a Manger*, in the word "lowly." "Squirrel-nimble" by its rhythm suggests anything other than night, and this may have encouraged the poet to add "And star" so awkwardly hung over into the next line.

> *And star: held and blessed, though you scour the high four*
> *Winds, from the dousing shade, and the roarer at the latch,*
> *   cool in your vows.*

Here, however, the escape from Sussex weekend sentimentality is managed only by an escape into the grosser sentimentality of *hwyl*. There would seem little need for "blessed" after "grace," and one is unsure whether "held" means someone holds her in his arms, or whether it means "kept close" by the cottage. But now this girl lying in "grace," "blessed," "under linen and thatch," "*scours* the four winds" from the "*dousing* shade" and the "*roarer* at the latch," yet remaining "cool in her vows." These are the consequences of what I mean by deficiency in realization—how can one respond to the feeling of a girl "under linen" ("sleep spelled") involved in "scouring" (from "dousing") or lying under the "star," in a "squirrel-nimble grove" with the "roarer" at the latch, yet remaining "cool"? If one could respond it would be to emerge somewhat exhausted from what promised to be a quiet night. Again, "Yet out of the beaked, web dark and the pouncing boughs," while one knows what is meant, the poetic texture jars unpleasantly on the nerves. For "beaked," while suggesting birds' beaks in the dark wood seen, and by its sound the tearing beak of owls; and "web" the unpleasant expectation of cobwebs clammy on one's face in the dark—yet both by their association suggest something quite the reverse of uncanny, like ducks or geese.[2] The suggestion is of fears in a still night: and one would then expect boughs which (as to a child) look as if they are clutching hands: but here the boughs *pounce*, which they only do in a very rough night: *pounce* because of its plosive sound has a very vigorous rhythm, and contrasts badly here with the little squeak of *beaked*: which suggestion is one to take? Certainly if the boughs are pouncing and the roarer is at the latch there would be no difficulty in seeking *a way sly and sure* without being heard. Did Dylan Thomas *see and feel* his Thief finding his way through the dark wood? The rhythm and texture reveal he did not: the poet's arms, as it were, are waved in the direction of realization, but the exact voice cannot be heard, no exact rhythm of experience taken, no definition.

Apart from the regular five-beat scheme Dylan Thomas uses a four-beat scheme (e.g. "The tombstone told when she died") to which I feel my comments on the five-beat line equally apply—there is too little flexibility to wrest the pattern to an organic shape. Never is he governed by the exactitude in flexibility by which Hopkins—as we know from his letters on sprung rhythm—disciplined himself most severely. Thomas worked on his verse, but from the outside—the rhythmical life was mostly never therewithin. A crude pattern on which roughly to lean his feet is more important to him than the wayward rhythm of the actual experience.

A more flexible pattern is used for one or two of Thomas's more successful personal poems. There is in these a mounting tumbling rhythm that sustains a mood. Yet it is contained by no structure save that of the system of line-breaks and, again, the five-beat rock-bottom blank verse line. If one writes the stanzas out as prose there is no natural rhythm from which one could rediscover the stanza pattern:

> Pale rain over the dwindling harbour and over the sea-wet church the size of a snail with its horns through mist and the castle brown as owls but all the gardens of spring and summer were blooming in the tall tales beyond the border and under the lark-full cloud. There could I marvel my birthday away but the weather turned round.

Indeed, when one has done that, one sees the writing-out-into-lines as merely to present as poetry what is, in fact, not even very good prose, despite its exciteableness. Once it is "poetry," that is, the vagueness and carelessness of expression tend to be accepted by us, because of the breathless *hwyl*. Yet what is there so striking about "the castle brown as owls"? Does he mean church and castle brown as owls, or the castle brown as an owl—but is unwilling to have the implication of shape and other qualities this way of putting it would have rendered? Did the castle look like *owls* or an *owl*?

What are the "tall tales"? Are the plants in the gardens "tall tales"? Or are the tall tales those in his imagination and delight in "his shower of all my days"? Where then is "beyond the border"? We are not meant to ask. The tumbling rhythm carries us past the demand for meaning. (For further discussion of this poem see the latter part of this chapter.)

Indeed it is possible to substitute any other set of words in a poem: the verse will still sound like Dylan Thomas:

Flash hawk over the wrangling hedges
And over the fire whack cloud the loft of a dab
With its sedge through hens and the willow
Grave as birds
But all the herons
Of psalms and shadows were sailing in the white cranes
There could I fable
My sailing
Away but the river turned around. . .

All I have done is substitute random words from *Over Sir John's Hill*. The rhythm, a dead frame, remains, and the meaningless verse looks exactly like Dylan Thomas's poetry. But the exercise exposes, too, the complete absence in his poetry of "inscape," organic rhythm, pattern, the true voice of poetry. And they are absent because there is no metaphorical discipline of exploring reality by art. It is all word-game, infantile babble, and as disarming as that.

Fern Hill represents, I feel, the best achievement of Dylan Thomas, because of its simplicity and the occasional breathless felicities of the rhythm: for instance:

And green and golden I was huntsman and herdsman,
the calves
Sang to my horn . . .

Where the line-break enacts the breathing into the horn; and again:

the hay
Fields high as the house . . .

where the alliteration of the "h's" enacts the breathless child's wide-eyed hyperbole and perhaps the scent of hay catching in the breath. But yet the poem relies too much on this its own impetuous childish rhythm: and the retrospect is not that of a man placing his childhood and his nostalgia for it, but characteristically of a man pitying himself for ever growing up:

> *Time held me green and dying*
> *Though I sang in my chains like the sea.*

Hence throughout there is a too-easy-come-by reliance on happy childhood words ("happy," "golden," "green," "it was lovely," "let me play," "young and easy"), invested with a good deal of wistful sentiment; while the adult attitude shows itself not in the texture and rhythm of self knowledge, but in verbal ingenuity—"once below a time," "in the mercy of his means," which remains merely ingenuity, word game; and in the religiose overtones which, meant to render the religious intensity of the child, are illegitimately employed to invest the child-self with the character of a saint or prophet, *hwyl*-wise:

> *And the sabbath rang slowly*
> *In the pebbles of the holy streams . . .*
>   *the spellbound horses walking warm . . .*
> *On to the fields of praise . . .*
> *blessed among stables . . .*

—the young Thomas, whom time has led by the hand up to the loft (whatever that may represent), is given us as the Christ child, Jesus-Thomas. The tumbling rhythm carries us quickly past this immature and dangerous egocentricity, here as elsewhere. If we pause, to bring up our touchstones, we shall find even *Fern Hill* evaporate into relative unimportance. When this happens, what is left?

Perhaps there is some justification for the acclaim of

Fern Hill in that an immature poet might be expecte
to deal with childhood with some success. *Fern Hill* is
a poem of nostalgia for childhood: but when we
compare it with Wordsworth, or with an example of
nostalgia in music, say Janáček's *On an Overgrown
Path*, we find it is a poem of seeking to revert to
childhood, rather than the placing of the impulse in
the man to revert. In Janáček the impulses ro re-
enter childhood are dramatically checked and placed
thus:

(from *On an Overgrown Path* Leoš Janáček, 1859–1928)

At the point indicated by an arrow, the composer says,
as it were, No! to the progress of the obsessional
movement of nostalgia, sinking through key-change to

key-change, back to childhood. At first *espressivo* and *dolce*, the middle section throbs towards a surging crescendo, which is deliberately broken by the one-eighth bar of rest, that the mature man may reconcile himself to the inaccessibility of the childhood world, by the controlling, if lamenting, sighing, main theme. Such control makes Janáček's pieces achieved works of art, conveying to us universal truths about the nature of growth in time, and the emotions of memory.

In Wordsworth we may find nostalgia placed by the tone of the words, by metaphorical enactment, and by the measured, restraining rhythm. Thomas bolts back to childhood on the steps of his rhythm. Wordsworth maturely ponders, recollects in mature tranquillity:

> I would record with no reluctant voice
> The woods of autumn and their hazel bows
> With milk-white clusters hung; the rod and line,
> True symbols of the foolishness of hope,
> Which with its strong enchantment led us on
> By rocks and pools, shut out from every star
> All the green summer, to forlorn cascades
> Among the windings of the mountain brooks.
> —Unfading recollections! At this hour
> The heart is almost mine with which I felt
> From some hill-top, on sunny afternoons
> The kite high up among the fleecy clouds
> Pull at the reins, like an impatient courser,
> Or, from the meadows sent on gusty days,
> Beheld her breast the wind, then suddenly
> Dash'd headlong: and rejected by the storm.

Here the nostalgia conflicts with many things: and, as in the music of Janáček, the ordering of the art is the ordering of the nostalgia: indeed the interest of the rhythm, movement, texture and imagery here is the interest of a developing grasp on life as the nostalgia is placed. To grow up, we need to recognize the reality of our own identity in the reality of the world, and this means taking in the flavour of Time and Death. If we can achieve this, we can attain a satisfaction, and a degree of order, that belong to the grown man. A hankering after the blisses of boyhood can be both a hankering for an impossible irresponsibility and a hankering after the perfection of heaven only glimpsed by the baby at the mother's breast, the perfect union of creatures—except that one creature is entirely dependent on the other, and cannot live its own life. Nostalgia of this kind implies the forfeiting of adult powers and satisfactions.

Wordsworth's poem does place the experience of nostalgia: he enters it knowingly, and thus placingly, to "record," albeit "with no *reluctant* voice": and the recording with its firm grip re-enacts and re-creates: "With milk-white clusters hung"—the consonantal energy is the energy of intense realization of the relished moment from the past. But the child's being lost in the intensity of living ("hung" with "clusters" suggesting the richness of the child's experiences) is placed in terms of the "rod and line" symbols of the "foolishness of hope. Which with its strong enchantment . . ." And he beautifully places, as a man, the child's intense absorption:

> shut out from every star,
> All the green summer, to forlorn cascades
> Among the windings of the mountain brooks.

And as he descends imaginatively into the quest of childhood along the brook he maintains his adult resistance: "Unfading recollections," "The heart is *almost* mine . . ." And in such lines as those famous ones from the *Prelude* about skating and about the rowing boat and the crag, one can feel the man's heart beating with, or as, that of the child, in the rhythm. But the heart is still that of the man, drawing on the feelings of significance, the experience, the grasp on life, of the child, yet placing the nostalgia and not using it for self-delusion or escape. Indeed, in the midst of the nostalgia, the release of childhood itself is a step towards maturity: the kite, in the movement of the lines, moves: its movement is studied and delineated by the man as a symbol of immaturity:

> . . . *then suddenly*
> *Dash'd headlong and rejected . . .*

—the ominous threat of nostalgia itself is placed here.

With Dylan Thomas, even in such a poem representative of his best and most articulate as *Fern Hill,* the reverse is true. In *Fern Hill* the childhood days are the "easy" "heydays," when the boy was "golden" and "honoured," "prince" of the "apple towns": the rhythm runs breathless to recapture what can never be recaptured. Here the nursery rhyme phantasy is employed to evoke the feelings of the experience of honouring oneself, and to indulge once more the feelings of infantile omnipotence (though this is placed a little by the wry, "And the sun grew round that very day.")

> *I lordly had the trees and leaves*
> *Trail with daisies and barley*
> *Down the rivers of the windfall light.*

The first stanza, technically speaking, is syntactically responsible, except for "Once below a time" whch is a whimsical departure—without true wit—from "once upon a time" in the way that a child might playfully alter the phrase: too much of Dylan Thomas's wordplay goes with his more general *enfant terrible* qualities—a whimsical wilfulness.[3] This is true of the "windfall light" which defines no aspect of experience meaningfully, however striking the failed metaphor may appear.

As the poem progresses we become aware of an increasing repetition which is at first insistent, then over-insistent: *green, golden, green and golden.* And a deepening religious note which, at first apparently the apocalyptic vision of the child, becomes merged into the child's self-honouring, and then becomes the childish self-worship of himself by the immature adult. Despite the whimsy of "once below a time," which is an attempt to place, the poet comes to identify himself with the child's self-worship, and falls into worship of his egocentric "noble" self: yearning, that is, for the complete selfishness only appropriate to, possible in, certainly only *acceptable* in, a child. In an adult such nostalgia can become a deathly limit on adult powers.

> *And the sabbath rang slowly*
> *In the pebbles of the holy streams,*

sets the religious note. The next stanza adds "it was *lovely* . . . it was air and playing, lovely and watering . . ." The *hwyl* develops in a rhythmical abandon along with an abandoned if intense vision that is uncontrolled by any placing of the immature experience by the man who finds maturity more satisfying. He simply accepts that it was "lovely" to be "blessed among stables," and invites us to share the disabling nostalgic indulgence.

In the fourth stanza "it was all shining" makes the "it was lovely" *hwyl* more deeply religious (it sounds better spoken with a Welsh sonority and passion) and not only does the adult poet take in the child's vision of creation, but gives it as his own:

> *So it must have been after the birth of the*
> *simple light*
> *In the first, spinning place, the spellbound horses*

> *walking warm*
> *Out of the whinnying green stable*
> *On to fields of praise.*

The last phrase is a fall to cruder religiosity, parasitic on the Magnificat and Genesis in the wrong way, and weak too is the "paradoxical" placing of "green" and "whinnying," applied as they are to the stable instead of the fields and the horses (sacrificing the vision to playful whimsy). Yet the first two lines are very fine: the collapse to a lower level is a consequence of the *hwyl* which disguises from the poet the poetic ambiguity of the imagery itself, which is of birth as well as creation and as such is related to his nostalgia: he yearns to be reborn, but *as a child*, not as a man. If one compares Thomas with Wordsworth, the rendering of this vision of creation as his own, not as that of the child is seen to show a cultivated immaturity. "Placing" by the mature sensibility is deliberately abandoned by allowing the rhythm to go out of control along with the meaning. And, of course, it is essentially this cultivated immaturity which makes Dylan Thomas popular: he avoids that pain of coming-to-terms with the conditions of life that maturity is: avoids, too, the need for an adult sense of order and responsibility, and the related search for order in language and responsibility to language.

Dylan Thomas here bemoans maturity, in terms of waking ". . . to the farm forever fled from the childless land"—except here, again, carelessness bedevils the meaning, as the attempt to double meaning leads to a confusion that yields no enrichening ambiguity— the line may mean either: "And wake to the farm (having) forever fled the land *of childhood*." or: "And wake to a farm which had fled forever from a land which was (is) now childless." Here the attempt to say something out of the ordinary by combining those two meanings has resulted in a meaningless confusion. The carried-away nostalgia for childhood is inseparable from a childish lack of organization in the verse.

Fern Hill is his most impressive poem, with such felicities as "My wishes raced through the house high hay" (which Vernon Watkins tells us the poet disliked) where even the affectation of omitting hyphens (it should be house-high) adds to the effectiveness, and the hay is both (by "raced") in the field and (by "house high") stacked.

However, Dylan Thomas's "slight delirium" prescription led elsewhere to an abrogation of the metaphorical power and rhythmical control that he shows in *Fern Hill* he could have developed. Never have powers been so disastrously thrown away: and that they were, belongs to the very immersion in the child attitude to experience from which *Fern Hill* springs. The terrible fact of Time which the poem approaches is essentially not met, because of the poet's self-protective absorption in pity for the Christ-like figure of himself-as-child:

> *Time held me green and dying*
> *Though I sang in my chains like the sea.*

Here again is the dissolving into meaningless, for nothing is less in chains than the sea, nor does the sea's noise, even in a tidal sound or on a beach, seem like "singing" in "chains." Perhaps, distantly, it may be true that the sea is in the chains of the moon's attraction, and "sings" when we listen to a sea-shell, but we cannot bring these images into focus with the "I" who is in chains and sings. Meaning dissolves here because there can be no meaning without approaching the truth, the reality Thomas "masks" himself against. We are all dying, as Mr. Eliot reminds us, "with a little patience . . ."—and his lines Dylan Thomas's echo. But the child is essentially dying into the man, a process necessary for life. Unfortunately for Dylan Thomas this death of the child to man proved unacceptable and his inacceptance leads to a deadening failure to mature:

> *The ball I threw when playing in the park*
> *Has not yet reached the ground . . .*

Thomas's rhythmical failure associates with his failure to accept maturity because of an obsessive nostalgia. And the whole lifelessness of this situation stultifies his metaphorical vitality—he cannot be metaphorically responsible because that would "carry him across" "the one-strand river" from childhood into adulthood.

For these reasons most of those poems of his which are not meaningless are what I would call "near-poems"—poems whose meaning breaks down at some point or other. The poems I would take to drive home my point about Thomas's "near-poetry" and his rhythmical failures would be the following:

The force that through the green fuse drives the
  flower (p. 9).

This poem gains some poetic life from its very denial of the natural world, conveyed in the rhythm as it drives over the first line-break. But the rhythmical progress of the first line conceals from us the falseness of the imagery: in what sense is the flower rising through the stem really like a burning fuse? It comes through a narrow stem, driven by natural forces, and "flames" out at the end: but the effect of "force"—"drives"—"fuse" is to evoke violence rather than resistance, and slow emergence.

After a while the apparent poetic argument—against growth—begins to disintegrate: "that blasts the roots of trees / Is my destroyer . . ." It may be that we could feel the flower as unwillingly driven through the "fuse" by force in time, consumed—but in no similar sense surely, are the roots of trees "blasted" by the natural force? The argument is being dictated, by false analogy: The flower is unwillingly driven through its fuse-like stem by natural force in time.—So am I growing.—The same force, as the spark reaches the end of the fuse, blasts the roots of trees and so destroys me. The weakness is in the extension of the fuse image into one of high explosive detonating, with little care for the metaphor, which here breaks down. It breaks down, because the impulse here is to justify a posture against natural growth in Time, because the poet wishes to pity himself for belonging to real natural processes, and dare not develop the responsible meta-phorical impulse to consider the mystery of natural growth as a universal experience, compassionately.

Thus the argument becomes less and less coherent. We may accept that in terms of universal images of flux, "the force that drives the water through the roots drives my red blood": but how the same force that "dries" the "mouthing" (? thirsty) streams turns mine (my blood or my mouthing?) to "wax" is incomprehensible.

And I am dumb to mouth unto my veins . . .
How at the mountain spring the same mouth sucks . . .

It is now difficult to grasp what this "force" is, if it "sucks" mountain streams and turns the poet's blood to wax. In the next stanza it becomes a hand—Nature's or God's—and it creates threats—the threats in external reality, whirlpools and quicksands. But why does the force "rope" the blowing wind and how is it that it "Hauls my shroud sail?" This is really an irresponsible pun, because a shroud is a rope, not a sail: the sail is meant to become a shroud, identified with the sail "hauled" by the "hand." We get the general sense — God, Nature or the Life Force both governs the winds and brings him to his death. But "ropes" diffuses rather than concentrates (perhaps because it is a vague echo of Herbert's "rope of sands").

In the next two lines he is not able to tell the "hanging man" (a Tarot touch from Eliot, and at the same time a touch of identification with Christ who is the "hanged man" in *The Waste Land*) that "of the same clay" of which his body is made "is made the hangman's lime." I see no point in this, except that it is a sensational way of referring to the unity of all flesh in clay, both murderer's, poet's and Christ's, and the clay which consumes all is itself compounded of all.

Now natural force in time becomes Time. We did not feel this established when the force was driving the green fuse and the "crooked rose" and "wintry fever" suggested life-processes rather than time. It is difficult to take Time as the driver of water, whirler of whirlpools, stirrer of quicksands, and hauler of ropes — the "force" and time seem at odds not with a true poetic complexity, but by a diffuseness of apprehension of experience. The "hanging man" image, for instance, is utterly gratuitous to the concept of the "force" which is also Time. Time, of course, brings the threat of reality and maturity which the poem is a desperate attempt by the poet to conceal.

Time sucks the blood of the fountain head (? by making us old and drying our faculties).

> *The lips of time leech to the fountain head;*
> *Love drips and gathers, but the fallen blood*
> *Shall calm her sores.*

The imagery becomes that of recoil from the bodily reality of love. "Gathers" means comes up to a boil or abscess, and the other images suggest menstruation

and (? venereal) disease if anything (drips and gathers—a boil is a "gathering") and are hideous—if we
respond at all, beyond the vaguest of impressions. The
violence of the recoil from the reality of sexuality and
of natural forces in maturing time is disguised by a
whimsical wordy gesture:

> And I am dumb to tell a weather's wind
> How time has ticked a heaven round the stars

Can this mean, as someone suggests, that "as time
ticks away, man constructs a heaven in space to
console him for the emptiness of space," and be a
near-Christian statement? Can "the fallen blood"
refer to Christ's blood? I cannot find anything so
graspable—to me this is nonsense, the "ticked," of
time, an impotent word to hang a "heaven *round* the
stars," even if to evoke the impotence is the point of
them.

> And I am dumb to tell the lover's tomb
> How at my sheet goes the same crooked worm

—the poem fizzles out with an echo from Webster.
The worm is "crooked" like the rose—why? Why
should he "tell the lover's tomb"? The "sheet" is a
winding sheet—why not "flesh"? Perhaps the poet
wanted to suggest the bed, with another gesture at
Blake's *Secret Rose* and its powerful sexual suggestions.

But the poem dissolves into mere gestures at the
poetic ("mouth unto," "at my sheet"). It is a near-
poem, existing only by its suggestion of unwilling
growth in the immature boy, "noble" ("And I am
dumb"!), and deserving of our pity *because* he is faced
with reality. But when we ask why he should be pitied
we seek in vain for the particular forms of metaphor,
rhythm, image, texture which convince us of a poet's
suffering. The language here is handled from the

outside, and thus lacks organic sap, as one can apprehend from its rhythmic deadness.

From love's first fever to her plague (p. 20).

A powerfully egocentric account of the poet's infancy, full of ecstatic *hwyl* about being at the breast. It gives the child's happy cosmic vision:

> *My world was christened in a stream of milk.*
> *And earth and sky were as one airy hill.*

Most of this poem assumes too readily that we are interested in being involved in the child-spirit's total vanity and self-aggrandizement (a psychiatrist would perhaps be interested in the way Thomas skilfully disguises his weaker chinks or in his rendering of the childish sense of omnipotence). There are some remarkable lines:

> *And from the first declension of the flesh*
> *I learnt man's tongue, to twist the shapes of thought*
> *Into the stony idiom of the brain . . .*

But, again, while this shows an unusual degree of thought for Thomas, the concept suffers from seeing the "twisting of thought" as external to the "stony idiom" of the brain to "shade and knit anew the patch of words." This suggests something happening to the outside, a manipulation of language, rather than a process rooted in the "idiom of the brain" itself. But the poem relates the urge to write in Thomas to the satisfactions at the mother's breast: it also, in its incoherence, gives clues to impress "Mummy"—and to recapture by fierce oral activity the ecstatic relationship: "One sun, one manna, warmed and fed . . ." This, of course, makes the poem psychologically interesting, but not interesting as poetry, with life to offer, from a living contest with experience, because it is too incoherent and lacking in "placing" organization to do that.

In this poem we have the essential clue: "The time for breast and the green apron age . . ." which dominates the verbal development. Words are manifestations of being alive:

> Left by the dead, who, in their moonless acre,
> Need no word's warmth . . .

And conversely, to lose verbal contact with the mother might be to lose warmth, and die. A separation fear binds Thomas to his babbling utterance: "one breast gave suck the fever's issue . . ."

'If my head hurt a hair's foot' (p. 97).

Thomas-worshippers will resent my placing this poem among the near-poems. But it seems to me a choice example of the urge to "make me a mask." The meaning relates to the birth of his own child, which is so unbearable that it is disguised out of existence. Thus there is no grasping or paraphrasing (I don't equate them) of such phrases as "if the unpricked ball of my breath/Bump on a spout let the bubbles jump out," "bully ill love in the clouted scene." Because it dare not be seen the meaning is not there, meaning which relates to the father's contest with the child for the mother's total attention. The painful imagery of pricking and throttling came from unconscious feelings of resentment—"pack back."

The child represents somehow a cross-claim to the wife's womb, which Thomas would have all to himself, as representing the lamented place where he was all to his own mother. He begins to write of the child as if the child were apologizing to the mother for hurting her in delivery—but the egocentric poet's voice takes over and the child's coming becomes a threat to his own possession of the same territory, and is resented. ("When you sew the deep door" is a reference to the father's possession of the birth passage.)

The child's birth is a reminder that when we are out

of the womb we are out, in reality, unto the grave. He echoes Hopkins's this is "no way to keep back beauty"—in life—"from vanishing away": "there is none, none, none . . ." But the cry is unresolved into any acceptance of mortality. He tells the child to rest in the "dust-appointed grain"—in the flesh which is appointed to come to dust, "At the breast stored with seas. No return . . ." Seas represent dissolution into the flux of matter. The voice is, at times, meant to be the voice of the mother. "The grave and my calm body are shut to your coming as stone . . ." But the disguising, "lie-shaping" voice of the poet breaks through. The second verse is thus quite without meaning, the poem full of images of neurotic recoil ("If my bunched monkey coming"), and extravagance. And the "mother's" voice offers advice to grasp reality in a form heavily weighted by the poet's own immature fears of it: "here you must couch and cry—" but the pity in the poem is for the poet himself, rather than the child, the prodigy who has been turned, now, as it were, out of two wombs. For the child there is a tone of prophesying doom: "And the endless beginning of prodigies suffers open . . ." This meaningless, though portentous-sounding line, disguises the fact that in welcoming the child the poet really wishes him dead— or in that reality which leads to the grave (which the endless beginning of prodigies suffers to open, as it suffers her body to open). He cannot accept that reality himself, though he must accept the reality of the child in it. But the poem is—

> Now to awake husked of gestures and my joy like a cave
> To the anguish and carrion, to the infant forever un-
>   free . . .

—the recoil, (as in the word "carrion"), the jealous, selfish hatred ("the infant forever unfree") the "an-guish" he wishes on the child-rival are concealed by

"husked-of gestures"—the whole poem, which bre...
down at many points, is an attempt to discover the
reality of the poet's feelings about birth—a valiant
attempt—but finding these feelings unexpressibly painful—asserts sentimental ones against them.

> Not for Christ's dazzling bed
> Or a nacreous sleep among soft particles and charms
> My dear would I change my tears or your iron head.

He is striving to accept the fact of birth against all his
unconscious resentments at the baby as a rival to the
mother-woman's affection. Thus, because it contains
opposing feelings, the meaning of the poem is unresolved, is diffused and contrary: it moves towards
compassion but is hampered by defence against insight.

A Refusal to Mourn the Death, by Fire, of a Child in London (p. 101).

This poem is generally considered to be one of
Thomas's best. The poem is a refusal to mourn which
in fact takes the form of an extensive mourning; we
thus have something similar to *After the Funeral* in
which good reasons are given for avoiding an exhibi-
tionist display of feeling, only to be discarded, in
favour of the display itself (see Chapter 3). Here the
refusal to mourn the child is apparently an even more
noble thing to do than mourn because it implies
restraint. Yet this is made the excuse in fact for
complete lack of restraint—a lack of restraint which
does not prevent the emotional attention the poem
demands flowing rather towards the "bard on the
raised hearth" than towards the child.

He says (at three stanzas' length) that he will not
say anything "further" about her death until he is
dissolved into the flux of matter. Though why he
shouldn't say anything is not clear, unless he is disguis-

at there is a "grave truth" in his true
...re which he is withholding in favour of
...play. The last verse is really general and
...guise of feeling in *hwyl*: how profound
...ast line, "After the first death there is no

...is worth paraphrasing so we may ask
ourselves what it gains by being verse at all:

> I will not utter any further elegy of the innocence and
> youth of this child. I will not blaspheme against the mys-
> tery of her dying by using my breath for this, taking up
> postures, as works of art do when, for instance, they
> dwell on the stations of the cross, lingering on suffer-
> ing.[4] She was human and she went—as mankind does,
> and I shall not murder this human act of dying by spin-
> ning "grave" truths out of it, universal and lofty com-
> ments. Her death was majestic enough: she burned.
>
> I will not let my tears fall like seeds in the least valley
> of sackcloth (? where they may grow into larger self
> inflicted griefs) or make the least shadow of a sound of
> prayer—never, until the world ends.
>
> Then the darkness which makes mankind, which
> fathers birds, beasts and flowers, and humbles all,
> will tell with silence that the last hour of everything
> is breaking, and the sea is forever to be still which now
> is always tumbling in its harness of wind and tide. Then
> I shall enter, as matter in the flux of matter, the holy
> land of the bead of water, the temple of the ear of corn.
>
> (The imaginative logic here is surely false, for, when
> everything passes away there are no beads of water nor
> ears of corn even for dead poets to enter into?)
>
> Deep with all dead, even the first dead, lies London's
> daughter, attired in the long companionship of matter
> (? I only suppose this is what "long friends" means), the
> ageless fragments of molecules, the dark flux of mother
> earth, hidden by the indifferent water of the flowing
> Thames. When we have died once we do not die again.

A gesture at accepting reality, the poem loses itself

in *hwyl*-afflatus, and disguises the essential underlying fear of death that is evoked in the poet. Flowing with no compassion for the child the metaphorical content of the poem is hollow and dead. Of course, it *sounds* magnificent, and is one of the best possible examples of concocted poetry. As poetry, the afflatus and incantatory rhythm and voice add nothing to the paraphrase, except to involve us in an extravagant gesture which gains its sentimental force by deprecating gesture while trying to deny death by magic.

Poem in October (p. 102) is a true poem, but we may raise the same objections to its dealings with reality as we may to *Fern Hill*. An ecstatic rhythm whose roots are in a personal self-deception attempts to recapture, in nostalgia, the elation of the child. The rhythm is not that of the adult check of nostalgia, but the tumbling, open-mouthed, urgent, nostalgic wish to re-enter childhood again, unbridled. Thus, necessarily, it must go dead, since the wish is an impossible one, leading further away from the difficult search for adult personal reality and awareness which is the true basis of poetry.

They may be accepted as light sentimental yearnings for lost innocence, but only if we accept the part lie of wishing "I could":

> Could I marvel
> My Birthday
> Away . . .

Sometimes there is little reason why the verse of *Poem in October* should not be in prose, except that in prose it would not be so playful—the extravagance weighs the argument in favour of our acceptance of the man-as-child.

> . . . and saw so clearly a child's forgotten mornings when he walked with his mother through the parables of sunlight and the legends of the green chapels and the

twice-told fields of infancy that his tears burned my cheeks and his heart moved in mine. These were the woods the river and sea where a boy in the listening summertime of the dead whispered the truth of his joy to the trees and the stones and the fish in the tide. And the mystery sang alive still in the water and singingbirds. And there I could marvel my birthday away but the weather turned around. And the true joy of the long dead child sang burning in the sun. It was my thirtieth year to heaven stood there then in the summer noon though the town below lay leaved with October blood. O may my heart's truth still be sung on this high hill in a year's turning.

Printed thus as prose the poem is tearful and flat, like Patience Strong, despite its remarkable "placing" advance in at least seeing the child in him here as "him" ("his tears burned my cheeks") rather than "me." The repetitive "and the" "and the" shows the poet inflating, exacerbating his own nostalgic indulgent *hwyl*, and the poem ends in a tearful mood of self-pity—"may I still be here next year"—poor me, who has had to grow up.

The value of the poem is in its evocation of the town and its atmosphere. The effect of the "mystery" and "marvels" too is not without effectiveness and not entirely without some "placing" as belonging to the child's rarely capturable vision. The effort of "marvelling" the birthday away despite the incantation is almost an acceptance of age itself, and this explains the moderate success of the metaphorical life of this poem.

Once below a time (p. 132).

One of the strange characteristics of Dylan Thomas is his complete lack of humour when writing his "scatter-breath" poetry glorifying the child, or speaking as a child-in-glory. This, of course, is characteristic of the child-spirit, which can see nothing ironically comic about itself—cannot "place" itself, but must believe solemnly in its own grave mien. There are times when children cannot bear to be laughed at, and this marks a stage at or an area in which they are painfully uncertain of themselves. Even when Thomas offers himself self-consciously as in *Fern Hill* one is not quite certain whether to take such a line as "And the sun grew round that very day . . ."—is it an ironic rendering of the child's belief, or an attempt to recapture and indulge in the child belief?

In this poem he gives us a picture of himself, whimsically (as suggested by "once *below* a time"), but lacking in humour, as a naughty, but exceptionally prodigious, boy:

The bright pretender, the ridiculous sea dandy . . .
  with his pretty penis exhibited to the world—
With my cherry capped dangler green as seaweed . . .

It would be all very endearing, if it were not so solemn at times: "Never never oh never to regret . . . (the bugle I wore)." The child's egocentric needs for exhibitionism are indulged in for their own sake, approvingly—"Now shown and mostly bare I would lie down . . ." And, certainly, after reading so much of this "look at clever little me" poetry of Thomas one becomes as irritated as with a real child's insistent claims for attention, only more irritated, because Thomas is an adult and ought not to find such wild childishnesses so portentously significant. A child who bothered one so, to see it "shown and mostly bare" would be spanked, not for its exhibitionism, but for being a pestering nuisance. (One feels the same about that other adult infant, Henry Miller.)

Among those killed in the Dawn raid was a Man Aged a Hundred (p. 135).

Dylan Thomas's war, as far as his poetry goes, seemed

to be merely an unusual opportunity for poses
struck over unusual victims. Just as his Wales is a
toy-town Wales, so his war is largely a toy-war. The
truly suffering Wales, of the valleys of detrition from
Ebbw to Dowlais, the hideous vulgarity of Welsh
suburbia, the formlessness and inhumanity below the
hill farms, the Baedeker bombing of Cardiff—these
escape him.[5] So did the suffering behind the million
ordinary careworn sleepless faces of bombed English
cities, and the savagery of human evil in conflict. All
his war poems do is to erect elaborate memorials to a
few victims, selected, as the gutter press would select
them, for sensational interest; for him they serve to
lead our attention to the "noble" author. The memorials are decorated with a fair amount of extraneous
comic extravagance—representing "universality": there
is something hard and mean—or emotionally inadequate—in clowning thus over violent death. Thomas's
clowning is a form of schizoid self-defence against the
reality of death.

What does this poem say?

*When the morning was waking over the war
He put on his clothes and stepped out and he died . . .*

The pat rhythm seems evidence of superficial feeling.
Why "over the war"? It should be "during the war"
but "over" sounds more poetical, and comes presumably by a cold-blooded manipulation of "over the
wall," in external word-play, "the morning was waking over the world."

*The locks yawned loose and a blast blew them wide,
He dropped where he loved . . .*

"where he loved" is merely a juggle with "where he
lived"—adding a meretricious poignancy to

*on the burst pavement stone
And the funeral grains of the slaughtered floor . . .*

These are Thomas clichés—"grains" for molecules. And here are the Thomas slack or whimsical habits of verbal combination—"slaughtered floor" for "the floor on which he is slaughtered"; "funeral grains of the slaughtered floor" for "deathly bits of blasted pieces of the pavement floor on which he was slaughtered and where he now lies disintegrated"—these habits in fact diffuse and loosen the texture of the language, making the rendering thinner and more imprecise than prose.

"Tell the street on its back . . ." Why "on its back"? Because the houses are flattened? ". . . he stopped a sun . . ."—as in "he stopped a bullet"? Stopped a bomb blast? "And the craters of his eyes"—"craters" because he is lying dead in a crater: a joke pun. "Grew springshoots and fire—"flames coming out of his eyes, while he heard the popping effects of blast: "When all the keys shot from the locks and rang." On violent sudden death this playful nonsense seems repulsive and shows a childish ineptitude of feeling. Had Thomas ever felt what it is like, or imagined what it feels like to be near a bursting shell or blast of high explosive—the instant helpless horror of being at the mercy of merciless forces—he could not have played with words so ineptly over such a theme. A poet should, by negative capability, be able to realize such pain and fear. Such a poem as this inhibits the mature flux of human emotion, it is too uncompassionate.

"Dig no more for the chains of his grey-haired heart." The cold-blooded image of watch-chain mixed with his hair and shattered heart is inept. It is the ineptitude of clever ad.-language when it attempts the larger theme. "The heavenly ambulance drawn by a wound"—the "wound" comes so often and so vaguely in Thomas—there is hardly a poem without the word —it is difficult to know what it does mean here, where in fact it probably means just "a wound."

But how is it the ambulance "Assembling waits for the spade's ring on the cage"? Both are meaningless lines, except perhaps insofar as they convey the sound of a shovel digging a grave or shovelling up the bits of corpse. The "common cart" is "Shakespearean":

> O keep his bones away from that common cart,
> The morning is flying on the wings of his age
> And a hundred storks perch on the sun's right hand.

Pity, sorrow, bewilderment, anger—all such real feelings are absent and the clue is in the lifeless rhythm— there is only the Laertes-like posture, the acted pose, "O I am out!" And the effervescence of a tinsel childish imagination: a hundred storks, perched on the sun's right hand. In the absence of deep committed feeling, the poem seems coldly calculated display, merely. We need only to compare the acute realism, penetrating and compassionate, of the description of Stevie's dismembered body in Conrad's *The Secret Agent*, or the shouted phrase in Lawrence's *Odour of Chrysanthemums*, " 'E wor smothered!," to know what the mature artist's treatment of death can be in compassion.

In *Lament* (p. 174) we reach the end of the solemn child-babble of noble attitudes struck, the self-deceit of religiose banter—disguising the absence of the true voice. Here these become their inversion. The Thomas who has represented himself as a naughty wild boy exposing himself bare to the sea, but eminently deserving of mother love for his Christ-like omnipotence and prodigiousness, becomes the cynical apologist for his own self-destructive inability to live, to accept his personal reality. Here is the Thomas of *Under Milk Wood*, of "Came to a bad end: very enjoyable," "What will you have?—Too much": and the final disguise of inward suffering: he is his own answer to these special pleas.

Here, "And all the deadly virtues plague my death—" concludes the poem with a pointless inversion of morality: people (the poem implies) love to sin— virtues are hollow, inadequate, and less than the reality:

> Chastity prays for me, piety sings,
> Innocence sweetens my last black breath
> Modesty hides my thighs in her wings

—but like the small boy in *L'Enfant et les Sortilèges* the protagonist cries "*Je suis méchant! Méchant et libre!*"

In the adult who is deficient in reality sense, there is a capacity to devote huge energies to making special pleas for tolerance of his shortcomings—pleas which do not bring forth the compassion we should feel, but which disarm us from supposing there is anything wrong at all, establishing an atmosphere of amorality—the intention is to involve us in the "wickedness" and secure our approval. This poem does these things. It has its parallel in the disturbing plea for the Cherry Owens and Polly Garter in *Under Milk Wood*: the contempt for others, for the "good" life, is unconcealed: there is even a kind of cruel sneer:

> I could love and leave
> All the green leaved little weddings' wives
> In the coal black bush and let them grieve . . .

And the appeal of the poem is in its dirty-joke allusions, "wick-dipping moon," "the sizzling beds of the town cried Quick!," and "black bush." "Wherever I ramped . . . I left my quivering prints."

The use of the ballad form is a further attempt to involve our sympathy in matter which is essentially cruel and amoral—full of insolent, contemptuous and untender attitudes to women. Here the "affirming" Thomas joins in the schizoid attack on human nature, with those like Miller and Durrell, who must affront the life they fear. In this coarse ballad *Lament* Dylan Thomas makes his capitulation as artist, his denial of the reality of good, and his sick plea for tolerance of that egocentric desperate sensuality of the child which eventually killed him: "Now I am a man no more no more." The collected poems thus end at the level of the Ballad of Sam Hall, the obscene Army song, the hero who "only had one ball," the savage negative cry of "Damn his eyes, blast his soul . . ." but here without the bitter weary irony of the Army lewdness, and with an artificial rollicking quality that is nearer to Newbolt:

> And a black reward for a roaring life . . .
> For, oh, my soul found a Sunday wife . . .

The destructiveness is disguised by the heartiness and the clowning whimsy, as in *Under Milk Wood*: "Isn't life a terrible thing, thank God?"

The incomplete last *Elegy* is a final attempt to see himself as a pitiful man who

> Above all he longed for his mother's breast
> Which was rest and dust . . .

There could be no better elegy for Dylan Thomas, for his inability to leave seeking his mother's breast—that impossible degree of heavenly rest and security for the mature man—brought him to the dust, in his prime. And in this near-poetry, of a rhythmic deadness, and incompleteness, with roots in that urgent need to babble a way back, self-destructively, to the mother's breast is found his near-achievement.

Out of the sighs a little comes . . .
A little comes, is tasted, and found good . . .

AT TIMES, in spite of everything he was encouraged to
become by his world and his associates, Dylan Thomas
reveals a very deep personal suffering, and the struggle
of an immature spirit to grasp the mature reality
without acceptance of which he knew unconsciously
he must die.

Thomas was not entirely without self-knowledge,
and the intuitive self-critical power of the artist. This
awareness he expresses from time to time, albeit with
fear. Here is a poem quoted by G. S. Fraser in *Vision
and Rhetoric* in which he does this.

I have longed to move away
From the hissing of the spent lie
And the old terrors' continual cry
Growing more terrible as the day
Goes over the hill into the deep sea;
I have longed to move away
From the repetition of salutes,
For there are ghosts in the air
And ghostly echoes on paper
And the thunder of calls and notes.

I have longed to move away but am afraid;
Some life, yet unspent, might explode

> *Out of the old lie burning on the ground,*
> *And, crackling into the air, leave me half-blind.*
> *Neither by night's ancient fear,*
> *The parting of hat from hair,*
> *Pursed lips at the receiver,*
> *Shall I fall to death's feather.*
> *By these I would not care to die,*
> *Half convention and half lie.*

Mr. Fraser says that in these lines Dylan Thomas is refusing to cut himself away from the tangled lines connecting himself with his childhood fears and phantasies. But I find it indicative that the poetry comes, in as far as it means anything, almost to have a surprisingly alien honesty here for Thomas: as Fraser says, the lines show insight. Significantly, what the poet fears is "life" bursting from the unspent burning old "lie"—he fears, that is, the release of his life from the misrepresentation of it. It is as if he dare not, in the nightmarish imagery, move away from his own self-spun neurotic tangle. Yet, with the insight he shows in these lines, he can yet *wish* to "move away" from "the repetition of salutes" and the "ghostly echoes"—the pretend-world of his own poems. In these last phrases he is describing his poetry as I would describe it. Significantly, the refusal to "move away"—which would be a move into maturity—is made a refusal to die, just as, in *In Country Sleep,* the Thief is Time, Death, *and* the reality of Maturity. Perhaps the most remarkable appropriateness of these lines is their image of the "spent lie" as a pyrotechnic affair.

His poetry itself *is* fireworks, often to disguise the very reality by which the poem was first inspired. Yet what he fears here is the real life burning in the old lie. The poem dissolves into nonsensible statements: but it seems to me an approach to a fear underlying all his work—the fear of the poetry itself touching his personal reality, and bringing it order and release. As the neurotic patient fears, in psychoanalysis, sometimes, that he will die if certain centres of resistance are touched and unravelled, so Dylan Thomas fears death by the forces of life itself. He fears death in maturity, as in *In Country Sleep*, and he fears death in the reality of love itself.

The irrational fears in this poem are the kind we preserve from childhood, if we are neurotic, of spiders or thunderstorms. And like a child he wishes to walk away from the burning firework, but dares not, remains there spellbound. The adult "salutes" of raised hat, pursed lips in expressions at the telephone receiver, seem themselves meaningless and deathly, empty gestures like the "spent" lie which although it burns pyrotechnically is essentially empty. All these magical gestures in life, like the ghostly echoes on paper, his own poems, seem threatening, because some old life in them might suddenly half-blind him, or kill him. He would not want to die by something which was half conventional, like the lift of a hat, or half untrue, like an empty poem: he means he knows that these, any more than the fear of night, can't in fact kill him. But like the child whose neurotic fear half-tells him he must not walk on the cracks in the pavement, he is taking no chances.

And taking no chances, obviously, meant more often than not failing to "move away" from the "repetition of salutes." The poem, confused and strange, is an emanation from the poet's very impotence itself, a fear of writing poetry which would begin to touch his reality, and lead him somewhere, away from the fascinated horror of childhood fear. Like King Lear, he preserves his attention on the feather which tells us whether we are still alive or no. Like a child Thomas preserves his belief that there must be a feather at our nose before we are dead—until then we can keep up the appearance that we are not. So long as there is no unstirring feather, the raising of hats, the fear of night, the fascinating hissing firework, the ghost on paper, *the poem* itself, will not be able to kill us.

In such a poem we can feel the degree of suffering in a soul so subject to the pressure of childish neurotic fears that it cannot even write the poetry which could offer a means to self-organization.

A similar poem is the following (p. 63):

> *Should lanterns shine, the holy face,*
> *Caught in an octagon of unaccustomed light,*
> *Would wither up, and any boy of love*
> *Look twice before he fell from grace.*
> *The features in their private dark*
> *Are formed of flesh, but let the false day come*
> *And from her lips the faded pigments fall,*
> *The mummy cloths expose an ancient breast.*
> *I have been told to reason by the heart,*
> *But heart, like head, leads helplessly;*
> *I have been told to reason by the pulse,*
> *And, when it quickens, alter the actions' pace.*
> *Till field and roof lie level and the same*
> *So fast I move defying time, the quiet gentleman*
> *Whose beard wags in Egyptian wind.*
>
> *I have heard many years of telling,*
> *And many years should see some change.*
>
> *The ball I threw while playing in the park*
> *Has not yet reached the ground.*

The last two lines admit the persistent immaturity, poignantly: the previous two the failure to change in the direction of accepting reality and wisdom. The terrifying opening lines, in all their incompleteness, their guilty morbidity, attribute to the "holy face" the withering disapproval—Freudian psychodynamics calls the super-ego, a censorious presence in the unconscious, which restrains the spontaneous impulses from the heart and pulse. The significant lines are those about "her lips," "the mummy cloths" and "the ancient breast": the unrecognized unconscious obsession is with the mother's breast which is "rest, and dust": this image it is which obscures the "change" which "many years" should have brought.

The truer poems of Dylan Thomas are those which deal with his own inability to speak as he wished to speak. *Our Eunuch Dreams* (p. 14) is a successful poem because it approaches a fusion of feeling and thought—a pondering of the infertility of our popular culture. With this thought goes a measure of self-knowledge. It seems to me to represent the kind of poem from which Thomas could have gone on to write true poetry. The thought is consistent, and the relationship of the experience to it exact. The stumbling blocks are the eccentric, sensational, delineations—of adolescent erotic dreams as necrophiliac (Thomas's may have been, of course), of physical love as "cures" of "itch," and the "being loth." These express only personal disabilities, as of a preoccupation with the "lost" mother which inhibits mature love. But the poem is courageous in its positiveness—only discipline and suffering awareness could have taken the poet further, in exploring his antipathy to the reality of love suggested in this poem.

The offence to the dead in the poem, "kicks the buried from their sack," is hysterical and weak: and the concluding "And we shall . . . / And who . . ." are a false hortatory conclusion from something not metaphorically proven or explored. But the poem has an interesting rhythm:

> Which is the world? Of our two sleepings, which
> Shall fall awake . . .

Despite the slight verbal carelessness ("grafts on
its bridge" is a callow gesture) it suggests a true controlled voice which Thomas, the gabbler, could have
had: it seeks, in its control, towards the joyful acceptance of sexual love as what we must "have faith" in.

Another "true poem" is *Out of the sighs* (p. 48). In
these poems of his true voice Dylan Thomas reveals
remarkable self-knowledge of his own proclivity for
evading his own approach to personal reality.

> Out of the sighs a little comes
> But not of grief, for I have knocked down that
> Before the agony . . .

Sadness he can bear: but grief he "knocks down"
before it becomes an agony. (The grief is something to
do with the "lost" mother.) The "knocking down"
could be done either by writing, fiery near-, or non-
sense-, poetry, or by violence on the self,

> the spirit grows,
> Forgets, and cries:
> A little comes, is tasted and found good;
> All could not disappoint . . .

What "comes" is joy, satisfactions in life, in love or
poetry, out of the spirit's process of growing, forgetting
(the grief which has been "knocked down") and
crying. But the little that comes is enough to give some
certainty for which there is gratitude.

Certainty of what? This poem gives us a glimpse of a
hell of not being able to seize one's personal reality:
permanently defeated from that, and so barred from
"loving well" as a mature man, he has to be content
with a negative certainty if only of that truth. Here the
linguistic awkwardness takes us for once to the elusive
disconnection of the soul in Thomas, to the root of his

problem, and the rhythm is the unpretentious, unges-
turing one of a man's self-contemplative voice:

> *There must, be praised, some certainty,*
> *If not of loving well, then not,*
> *And that is true after perpetual defeat.*

The omission of "be" in "There must, be prasied, [be]
some certainty" to make the line even in rhythm and
the simplicity of "then not,"/"And that is true" are
the simplicities of a voice, like Hamlet's at times,
soliloquizing on the borders of madness. But in its
sorrow it is a voice with true rhythm.

> *After such fighting, as the weakest know,*
> *There's more than dying:*

—the inward hell can be worse than death

> *Lose the great pains or stuff the wound,*
> *He'll ache too long.*

To lose "the great pains" is to enter the oblivion of
anaesthesia, for this poet the anaesthesia of alcoholic
stupor in life, or *hwyl* in poetry. Other measures to
heal are rejected—kindness, personal therapy, cures,
love.

> *Through no regret of leaving woman waiting.*
> *For her soldier stained with spilt words*
> *That spill such acrid blood.*

I may be myself here engaged in the common process
of using Thomas's language to attach to it the meaning
I want the words to have. But here I see "Through no
regret of leaving woman waiting" a reference to his
own fear of sex (as revealed in his poetry—and confined in his personal life) and of impotence—both
associated with the "weak" fighting of the soldier,
stained with "spilt" words: the soldier being a disguised symbol of his own impotent lack of sexual
"courage."

His words certainly are "spilt"—wasted—in futile battle with psychic horrors. And the word "spill" is repeated, while "spill such acrid blood" seems almost a critical reference to his own sensationalism in verse, and its similarity to useless physical waste of power. But the "bloody" sensationalism is both part of the agony, and the impotence—the woman is left "waiting" who should be "loved well." The flinching from sexual reality is a flight from all reality.

"Were the sensational wordy contest enough to ease the pain," he seems to say, "or was it enough to regret at the waste of words—then the self-deception of my happy childhood poems ["vaguenesses enough and sweet lies plenty"]—the hollow words themselves could bear all suffering, and cure me of psychic ills"—

> Were that enough, enough to ease the pain,
> Feeling regret when this is wasted
> That made me happy in the sun,
> How much was happy while it lasted
> Were vaguenesses enough and sweet lies plenty,
> The hollow words could bear all suffering
> And cure me of ills.

In such an unpretentious calm, true voice, what a true understanding of his own impulses! For here is a statement that the "verbal banter" is a means to allay intolerable anxiety ("enough to ease the pain") compulsively.

> Were that enough, bone, blood, and sinew,
> The twisted brain, the fair-formed loin,
> Groping for matter under the dog's plate,
> Man should be cured of distemper.

This man should be cured were that enough—the little that comes, of true self-awareness.

I would be cured of the twisted brain, he says, and of "Groping for matter under the dog's plate," that is, of seeking to disgust and looking for nastiness. The title *Portrait of the Artist as a Young Dog* gives the clue to his desire here expressed to be cured of the puppydom he, somewhere in his soul, hated and despised—are of the "distemper" which belongs to the Young Dog concept.

> *For all there is to give I offer:*
> *Crumbs, barn, and halter.*

The reference to "halter" is poignant: the collapse of the last stanza is the collapse of the confidence of "some certainty." The crumbs and barn are a gesture—not a posturing gesture, but a gentle one—towards humility. The ambiguity of "For all there is to give I offer" (For all there is I offer to give—or—For all one can give, all I can offer is . . .) makes it uncertain who is to give, the poet, or us. But for a moment the true voice breaks through to ask to be stilled from the mere "hollow words" of self-deception, and to be given, offering, a new start. Thomas was given the halter instead—the halter of his own babble, in which the world confirmed him, and the halter of his own self-destruction—for a halter is a traditional image of suicide.

It would be interesting to know under what circumstances these poems in which a true voice or partly true voice appears—*Should lanterns shine*, *I have longed to move away* and *Out of the Sighs*—were composed. At what points of personal balance was Thomas able to contemplate his predicament with some objectivity: and what turned the balance towards the false gabble again?

Perhaps the most revealing of the true poems is *O make me a mask* (p. 85). This is an important glimpse of the poet's poignant self-awareness of what he was doing by his more fake poetry.

> *O make me a mask and a wall to shut from your spies*
> *Of the sharp, enamelled eyes and the spectacled claws*
> *Rape and rebellion in the nurseries of my face . . .*

The rape and rebellion are the extravagance of verbal babble and sexual allusion, and the oral aggressive incantation against the acceptance of reality. These are "in" the "nurseries of my face"—they have their origins in the infancy of my personality. Also they come from my *mouth,* the nursery of my face, being that part of it which belongs to the nursing of an infant. (Here the ambiguity comes from the inside—is living metaphor.)

"O rape and rebellion" (the lines can be read) "make me a mask and a wall—to prevent people spying (the word is a betraying one) on my spirit." The "sharp enamelled eyes and the spectacled claws" is not a good line—the eyes should be spectacled and the claws enamelled—i.e. scholars and prying sophisticated women. The pointless transposition restores the disguise itself—belongs to the neurotic activity of avoiding the pursuing guilt and fear—the threatening, spying eye—by magical routines. This child-like magical routine (like walking in the squares and not on the lines) explains many of Dylan Thomas's apparently pointless word-swaps.

> *Gag of a dumbstruck tree to block from bare enemies*
> *The bayonet tongue in this undefended prayerpiece,*
> *The present mouth*

Alternatively by pretending to be inarticulate (the meaningless poems are also a form of dumbness) the tongue itself (which is unexpectedly like a bayonet) can be blocked from "bare" enemies in this "undefended prayerpiece," the "present" mouth. The fear now is of his own destructive power by language; by the inarticulateness itself he can be blocked from giving himself away by a sudden bayonet thrust of the tongue, leaving himself vulnerable, into a bare enemy. Here, obviously, verbal expression is related to sexual power, and fear of the incisive verbal thrust related to his fears of his own aggressiveness in sex, conceived of as making a wound in a bare enemy by bayonet. (This is perhaps how a disturbed child conceives of the sexual act.) The search to allay anxiety by verbal sensuality, as referred to here, is prevalent in present-day literature. It is a feature, for instance, of *Lady Chatterley's Lover* as a book and as a phenomenon. Psychotherapists like the late Melanie Klein would perhaps relate the oral (word) activity to the kind of anxious preoccupation with coition itself as a means to allay anxiety, by reassuring us that we are not impotent ("O God make me feel something. . . ."). If we could love adequately, then we would both stop talking so much about sex, and fall into a more unconscious rhythm in our sexual lives, without the need for constant reassurance of our potency by words.

Thomas's pain of exposure, by being "spied" on or thrusting, by words, is avoided by

The sweetly blown trumpet of lies,
Shaped in old armour and oak the countenance of a dunce

—avoided by the poetic archaisms, the baroque, externally-handled decoration of his verse. This simulates the countenance of a dunce. He is saying these are deliberate affectations, making "repro" poetry. "To shield the glistening brain and blunt the examiners." The brain "glistens," exposed, as with sweat in agony—the poet dare not expose his worst griefs—the examiners must be put off, fobbed, blunted:

And a tear-stained widower grief drooped from the lashes
To veil belladonna . . .

The "widower grief" means "affected" grief—but the implication that a "widower" is hypocritical reveals Thomas's unconscious preoccupation with the "dead" mother in the "widower"-father's place, expressed in many poems. Perhaps, even, the verbal bayonet is the desired sexual assault on the mother. But—significantly—we now approach matters only solvable by psychiatry and not criticism. Thomas's poetry, except where, as here, there are glimpses of a placing, ordering power, is raw material for psychoanalysis only, and not ordered by the powers with which the therapist, step by step, works.

In this poem O *Make me a Mask* the true poison of grief is to be hidden, and in the meantime the eyes, without tears, can watch others give themselves away —in responding to his poetry—lamenting their own deficiencies by lies, by the curve of the "nude" mouths—that is—without the cloaks of the guilt-accretions from "nurseries" or "bayonets"—or "the laugh up the sleeve"—pretend-laments.

The poem approaches a true vision of the reality of our literary world and Thomas's place in it—a world of "the laugh up the sleeve," "lamenting lies," "gags," and the "sweetly blown trumpet of lies." It is a complete account of Llareggub, and the dreadful suffering hidden beneath it, concealed by "the countenance of a dunce."

Under Milk Wood is described as a new departure by
Dylan Thomas, a literary development whereby "he
intended to turn from the strictly personal kind of
poetry to a more public form of expression, and to
large-scale dramatic works in particular, where there
would be scope for all his versatility, for his gifts of
humour and characterization as well as his genius for
poetry" (Daniel Jones, in the Preface). The work has
been staged, broadcast and recorded, and is widely
known. Its acclaim was accompanied by elegies on
Dylan Thomas by hands of some standing in the
literary world, and *Under Milk Wood* is taken to
represent the great things Thomas might have gone on
to write. ("It is fortunate that at least one of these
projected works has been preserved for us.") According
to the standards of our literary world, such as they are,
this play for voices is an achieved piece of some
distinction, even something towards a new poetic
drama. Particularly so, it is claimed, as it represents the
development of a new technique suitable for sound
broadcasting.

Under Milk Wood is the rendering of the life of a
small Welsh town by the sea from the middle of one
night to the middle of the next, by voices, and using
two commentators. The happenings in one spring day

in Llaregyb are recounted, by a kind of "dramatized" gossip. There is no main action, though there are episodes:

Captain Cat, a blind sea captain, dreams of his long-drowned mates, and recalls his happiness with the whore Rosie Probert whom he shared with the donkeyman.

Miss Price, dressmaker and shopkeeper, has an erotic dream of Mr. Mog Edwards, a draper who is courting her.

Jack Black the cobbler dreams of driving out sin, and makes his way abroad in the woods to seek the excitements of castigating the lewd.

Evans, undertaker, dreams of his childhood, stealing buns.

Mr. Waldo, a ne'er-do-well character, dreams of his mother, dead wife, other women he has slept with, and other sins, and in the end, is having intercourse with Polly Garter, drunk.

Mrs. Ogmore-Pritchard dreams of her two dead husbands, whom she has killed by hygiene.

The milkman dreams of emptying his milk into the river; the policeman urinates into his helmet by mistake.

Mr. Willy-Nilly, the postman, knocks on Mrs. Willy-Nilly's back in bed: "every night of her life she has been late for school."

Hour by hour as the town wakes up we go the rounds of the characters. Each character, or group of characters, is presented with a hardness of outline, and from the outside, like caricature—Llaregyb in this way is a kind of Toy Town.

The place itself bears no relationship to modern Wales, either in village or town—no such realistic relationship as Joyce's Dublin bears to Dublin. It is rather the toy-town of Thomas's childhood, and this is why he calls it "a place of love"—it is the place of his mother's love. The effect of the stylization of the piece is to make the world a pretend-place, with pretend-relationships, such as children play, with no morality or reality to impinge. Even Suzanne Roussillat sees that Thomas's Wales is not suffering modern Wales (not, of course, that it matters):

> Dylan Thomas sometimes mentions 'the cranes and the coaltips' so typical of the Welsh valleys; he never refers to his period of misery, or to the industrial activities of his home-country. It shows probably his attitude of complete detachment from any economical, social or political problems . . . Wales had nothing to offer a poet in those difficult years . . . (*Dylan Thomas, The Legend and The Poet*)

Making allowances for the difference between the function of the novelist who must be as inclusive as he can, and that of the poet, who, even if he writes prose, is bound to make his effect by economy of selection, this is Dylan Thomas's *Ulysses*. We have a similar use of characters' dreams, and, apparently, a similar investigation beneath the surface of outward appearance into people's motives and compelling inward drives as we have in Joyce. Again, in the comedy of rural life, in the approach to love and death in the small local community, where contemporary civilization impinges on vestiges of archaic social forms and values, we have something comparable with the work of T. F. Powys. Both with Joyce and Powys the rendering of local life is done to advantage by the use of a local idiom, and this is what Dylan Thomas too sets out to do. But as soon as one makes a comparison with writers of such gravity as Joyce or T. F. Powys the question arises— how seriously does Dylan Thomas intend his work to be taken? Has it a serious and valuable comment on experience to make?

The most successful passages in *Under Milk Wood* are those where an amoral playful vigour is in order, where the cruelty and solemnity of the child-spirit in Thomas is not maliciously drawn out, and where he is not making a special plea for his resistance to reality. The playful vigour can, indeed, establish a kind of humanity, revealing in its very babbling extravagance an ironic perception of the idiocies of adult antics:

SECOND VOICE   Mrs. Rose Cottage's eldest, Mae, peals off her pink-and-white skin in a furnace in a tower in a cave in a waterfall in a wood and waits there raw as an onion for Mister Right to leap up the burning tall hollow splashes of leaves like a brilliantined trout.

MAE ROSE COTTAGE [*Very closely and softly, drawing out the words*]   Call me Dolores
    Like they do in the stories

Here is a use of Joyce's ironic vigour which combines with the critical view Thomas showed himself capable of in *Our Eunuch Dreams*—critical of the adolescent's wild fantasies. It is his version of Joyce's pastiche of Gerty MacDowell's reading matter in the Nausicaa chapter of *Ulysses:* the sexual undertones, even ("raw as an onion," "a brilliantined trout") are appropriate—arise from the unconscious—and they satirise the onanistic intensity of the vision, comically expanded to the grotesque.

At times the writing employs Joyce's kind of control of language to good effect, to gain a rich comedy established by verbal play:

SECOND VOICE   He intricately rhymes, to the music of crwth and pibgorn, all night long in his druid's seedy nightie in a beer-tent black with parchs.

And there is much observation, too, of how people speak, and act—the rapid repartee of common life:

> she picks a posy of daisies on Sunday Meadow to put on the grave of Gomer Owen who kissed her once by the pig-sty when she wasn't looking and never kissed her again although she was looking all the time . . .

CAPTAIN CAT   Mr. Waldo hurrying to the Sailors Arms. Pint of stout with an egg in it

> [*Footsteps stop*]

[*Softly*] There's a letter for him.

WILLY NILLY   It's another paternity summons, Mr. Waldo.

FIRST VOICE   The quick footsteps hurry on along the cobbles and up three steps to the Sailors Arms.

MR. WALDO [*calling out*]   Quick Sinbad. Pint of stout. And no egg in. . . .

> There goes Mrs. Twenty-Three, important, the sun gets up and goes down in her dewlap, when she shuts her eyes it's night . . . who's dead, who's dying, there's a lovely day, oh the cost of soap-flakes . . .

MRS. BENYON [*Loudly, from above*]   Lily!

LILY SMALLS [*Loudly*]   Yes, Mum

MRS. BENYON   Where's my tea, girl?

LILY SMALLS [*Softly*]   Where d'you think? In the cat box? [*Loudly*] Coming up, Mum.

THIRD WOMAN   and going out fishing everyday and all he ever brought back was a Mrs. Samuels . . .

These are in the humane comic modes descended from Jonson and Elizabethan drama, expressive of low life and its vitality. The treatment of the Reverend Eli Jenkins, is, too, sympathetic and right, a caricature, but Dickensian and sympathetic: it has even a Dickensian movement:

SECOND VOICE   The Reverend Eli Jenkins, in Bethesda
House, gropes his way out of bed into his preacher's
black, combs back his bard's white hair, forgets to
wash, pads barefoot downstairs, opens the front door,
stands in the doorway and, looking out at the day
and up at the eternal hill, and hearing the sea break
and the gab of birds, remembers his own verses and
tells them softly to empty Coronation Street that is
rising and raising its blinds.

The Reverend Jenkins's poem is a good pastiche,
lightly satirizes and exactly catches the style of local
newspaper verse:

> *And boskier woods more blithe with spring*
> *And bright with bird's adoring,*
> *And sweeter bards than I to sing*
> *Their praise this beauteous morning.*

The sympathy is in the fact that Thomas does not
make him merely ridiculous. The other pastiche verses
are not so good—neither the children's game rhyme,
nor the sailors' song, nor Polly Garter's lament. But
Mr. Waldo's "Come and sweep my chimbley" is an
accurate rendering of the *double entendu* verse of
urban broadside balladry. And Thomas should be
praised for endeavouring to use the loose varied modes
of the Circe scene in *Ulysses*, for dramatic purposes.

Larger claims, however, have been made for this
work as one of the significant dramatic poetic works of
the last two decades, and here, surely, we must demur?
Considered in the light of the deeper moral functions
of art, *Under Milk Wood* is trivial. And, indeed, it is
really dangerous, because it flatters and reinforces the
resistance to those deeper insights we need. We need to
be able to allow our tender feelings to flow—*Under
Milk Wood* reinforces untenderness. It is a cruel work,
inviting our cruel laughter. We need to understand

love better—*Under Milk Wood* disguises and confuses. Indeed, once again, it makes special pleas for falsifications of the realities of personal relationships, as we shall see. All it may be said to have is comedy and linguistic exuberance: but these are derived rather from Joyce, often as quite direct borrowings, rather than rooted in any Rabelaisian vitality or Jonsonian irony that seeks to "correct manners" by the laying bare of human self-deluding pretensions. *Under Milk Wood* as light entertainment may be acceptable and even remarkable. As art it takes us nowhere, and merely flatters the prejudices of those who live in the suspended life of what Thomas himself called "the suspended pink marshmallow" of suburbia.

Sex, boozing, eccentricity, cruelty, dirty behaviour, are enhanced as subjects in a comic work, as *Under Milk Wood*, by the implicit background of suburban respectability, the interest lying in the daring naughtiness of their revelation. The norms, or the positives of living, expressed as the potentialities of human love, are absent: all human reality tends to be denigrated. Sometimes the denigration is relieved by humour, but only sometimes. And on the whole the breathless verbal patter is tedious. Why did the work become popular? The answer is that *Under Milk Wood* would not have had its popular success were it not essentially unreal and untender, and full of seamy hints, obscenities. The comparison with Joyce may be usefully pursued to help justify these pronouncements.

In *Ulysses* Joyce's positives are weak. Joyce's difficulty is to offer us positive values in human love without slurring into the sentimentality that one finds in his poems, *Chamber Music*. Yet behind Joyce's examination of the moral disintegration in contemporary life there is the courage of one who at least knows moral disintegration when he sees it, and fears the consequences for the European civilization to which he gratefully belongs. (The words "London—Zurich—Paris" at the end of *Ulysses* mean a good deal.) Joyce's positives are implied in the technique of the prose and his construction—the richness of the artist's verbal power, and the structural reference to classical antiquity. This is perhaps not enough, but Joyce certainly achieved and accepted the exacting responsibility of the artist, and his work has the power to deepen insight and enlarge understanding.

With Leopold Bloom, Marion or Stephen in *Ulysses*, in the brothel or at the adulterous riot in the bed at No. 7 Eccles Street, one feels a disturbing sympathy so that one despises or condemns them at peril of despising oneself. "There but for the grace of God, go I." But we laugh cruelly at Llaregyb, the "place of love"—because "we" are different from "them." This is how the child, cruelly, because it has not yet grown to the capacity to afford compassion, looks at the world. It is this infantile detachment from mature reality which this work reinforces in us.

But first, to examine the "technique." In its plan, as I have said—"a day in the life of a Welsh seaside town"—the play has an affinity with *Ulysses*. The technique derives with little originality, and too little understanding of Joyce's purpose, from the brothel scene in *Ulysses*. The only difference is the introduction of the first and second voices to give continuity: Joyce presents the dramatic fantasia without a *compère*.

In Joyce the technique of his brothel scene, the sequence of hallucinatory *montage* presented as if it were a dramatic episode with stage directions, was devised for a complexity of reasons. One is that in Night Town, and at a time when the chief characters are intoxicated or stimulated by feelings of lust, or anger derived from insecurity (Stephen is locked out), the situation naturally demands a bizarre and "unreal" rendering, like that of a stage or cinema set: it renders the sense of unreality of city night life. Again, in this section of the book the two groups of characters— those around Bloom and those around Stephen— draw together for the climax, again suggesting a dramatic rendering, as we have previously been in each chapter either "with" Bloom or "with" Stephen. Now, so that we may see their meeting at arm's length, we are given the dramatic spectacle, in which some scenes emerge from Stephen's mind, and some from Bloom's and some (which is a weakness) from the author's sheer delight in his own phantasmagoria. But the essential reason for the fragmentary and chaotic technique is that the writer renders here the climax of the fragmentary morality of the contemporary world, which permits no security of attitude to life, no governing moral complex, to Stephen or Bloom. That is their lamentable plight. Circe turns men into swine, but when they resist the simple transition and behave violently, she calls for the police: the irony of the passage is superb, and the very fragmentariness of the technique a controlling moral force. Joyce is able to explore, to present to us in the glaring arc-lights of his fantasy, some hideous and disgusting characteristics of contemporary life. Is it, as D. H. Lawrence said, "an *olla putrida* . . . old fags and cabbage stumps . . . stewed in the juice of deliberate journalistic dirty-mindedness"? At times, perhaps, the vibration is on the verge of obsession. But Lawrence is unfair even though it is true that Joyce's positives are far less assuredly present than those in Lawrence's novels. Within the whole pattern of *Ulysses,* here in the brothel scene Joyce is grossly humorous, but it is humour springing from a bitter irony and a courage of moral concern inbued with compassion for contemporary man. Lust, in the brothel scene, is rendered *as lust*, and associated with the imagery of physical revulsion. The vigour of Joyce's idiom—with its roots in English literature—preserves a positive reference to life, a hold, while destructive lust is ruthlessly explored.

To show how much lesser is his use of Joycean modes, Dylan Thomas's realization of the sea as a presence in *Under Milk Wood* may be compared first with passages from an earlier chapter of *Ulysses*. These are from Thomas:

> The sloeblack, slow, black, crowblack, fishing boat bobbing sea . . .
> the webfoot cocklewomen and the tidy wives . . .
> the jolly rodgered sea . . .
> the darkest-before-dawn minutely dew-grazed stir of the black, dab-filled sea . . .
> Captain Cat, the retired blind sea captain, asleep in his bunk in the seashelled, ship-in-bottled, shipshape best cabin of Schooner House dreams of

> SECOND VOICE   never such seas as any that swamped the decks of his *S.S. Kidwelly* bellying over the bedclothes and jelly fish—slippery sucking him down salt deep into the Davy dark where fish come biting out and nibble him down to his wishbone, and the long drowned nuzzle up to him . . .

And these from *Ulysses*:

> —God, he said quietly. Isn't the sea what Algy calls it: a grey sweet mother? The snotgreen sea. The scrotum tightening sea. *Epi oinopa ponton.* Ah Dedalus, the Greeks. I must teach you. You must read them in the original. *Thalatta! Thalatta!* She is our great sweet mother. Come and look.
> Wood shadows floated silently by through the morning peace from the stairhead seaward whence he gazed. Inshore and farther out the mirror of water whitened,

spurred by lightshod hurrying feet. White breast of the dim sea . . . wave white wedded words shimmered on the dim tide.

A cloud began to cover the sun slowly, shadowing the bay in deeper green. It lay behind him, a bowl of bitter waters.

The flood is following me. I can watch it flow past from here. Get back then by the Poolbeg road to the strand there. He climbed over the sedge and eely oarweeds and sat on a stoll of rock, resting his ashplant in a grike . . .

These comparisons are sufficient, I suggest, to show how derivative Dylan Thomas's poetic prose is, and also how little Thomas understood Joyce's genius. "Sloe black, slow, black, crowblack" in Joyce would have been concentrated into one word: in Thomas it is merely peppering the target without hitting the bull, and "fishing boat bobbing" is merely cliché, its movement in any case inappropriate, being too jerky. Joyce's rhythms relate closely to the feelings of experience. The associations of Thomas's "sloe" and "crow" are limited to their colours, maybe their sheen. In Joyce each chosen word reverberates always with other rich complexities: the mood of the protagonist, or the theme of the relevant chapter. Buck Mulligan's "snotgreen" and "scrotumtightening" not only convey the phsyical presence of the sea, but also render the desire to shock which is a characteristic of the medical student, and which offends Stephen deeply. The physical nausea and sexual offence of Mulligan's talk are set against that "grey sweet mother": Stephen is tortured by the feeling that he killed his mother by refusing to accept her faith on her deathbed, and he sees the round sea of Dublin Bay as the bowl of vomit by her on that occasion ("a bowl of bitter waters"). Similarly "light shod hurrying feet. White breast of the dim sea . . . wavewhite wedded words" . . . renders the complexity of Stephen's mood, the sea as a symbol of his mother, and the life of sex which repels him.

Joyce's words, then, are not simply chosen because of a "relish for language" or "music" separate from their meaning. His observation is perfect—compare that "eely oarweeds" in the next passage. But the local observation is rendered with the "native thew and sinew" of the language: like the language of Shakespeare's mature poetry, it develops both a local situation, a local mood, the present characters, and contributes to the wider poetic themes of the work. Dylan Thomas's "sloeblack," "crowblack," "jolly rodgered," "dab-filled" merely contribute to a "daft" cumulative effect of "atmosphere": "sloe," for instance, runs contrary, if one savours the word apart from its suggestion of colour, to the salt tang of the sea, and its infertility as against land and soil.

Again, while Dylan Thomas imitates Joyce's movement, he fails to learn from its subtlety of movement and rhythm. "The darkest-before-dawn minutely dewgrazed stir of the black, dabfilled sea" has a breathless rhythm that conveys an excitement but it is an excitement from which there is little relief in *Under Milk Wood*—it eventually becomes tedious, until the factitiousness of the energy becomes apparent. It goes with an emotional insecurity: we miss the controlled voice of the true creative understanding.

Joyce's cockle pickers actually do wade, stoop, souse and wade out *by the carefully punctuated movement*: "Cockle pickers. They waded a little way in the water, and, stooping, soused their bags, and, lifting them again, waded out." *Under Milk Wood* is deficient in any such controlled movement: the overladen, breathless patter of word relish becomes, after a while, destructive of our ability to take things in clearly and exactly: "The lust and lilt and lather and emerald breeze and crackle of the bird praise and body of Spring with its breasts full of rivering May milk . . ."

We may perhaps, still considering the "versatility" and "poetic power" examine further the much-praised opening pages of *Under Milk Wood*. There are, in those opening pages a number of truly comic phrases:

> like a mouse with gloves
> The Welfare Hall in widow's weeds
> the glasses of teeth
> the undertaker and the fancy woman

But there are also many phrases which, although sometimes cleverly turned, are clichés of journalistic writing:

> dickybird watching (people in all old photographs in cliché talk are "watching the dickybird")
> fishing boat bobbing (all fishing boats bob)
> cats . . . needling
> courter's and rabbits' wood (all Fleet Street woods are full of courting couples and rabbits)
> dewfalling
> invisible starfall (the night is also "starless")
> snuggeries of babies (woman's magazine babies are always snug)
> wetnosed dogs (actually Thomas with characteristic —and pointless—jugglery says "dogs in the wetnosed yards")

The picture is of a conventional village in conventional language, and the language used is subject to the same kind of external handling of words found in the worst kind of "clever" advertisement, which has no human purpose.

Besides these conventionalities there are many phrases which are simply meaningless: "quiet as a domino," "fast, and slow, asleep," "the muffled middle"—these, presumably, are the "poetic" ones, if only because we cannot understand them. Some phrases, like "dew grazed stir" only succeed with any inevitability. But the total effect of this "vitality" of language is in fact a deadness. It simply cannot be taken in: the impression it leaves is of no essential atmosphere, no flavour or quality, but an occasional felicity of caricature, a sense of ebullience, and an impression of "clever" writing. Night, for instance, in the first three pages, is said to be:

> starless, bible-black, having bucking ranches, be moving in the streets, be in the chill, squat chapel, be in the four-ale, quiet as a domino, be in Ocky Milkman's loft like a mouse in gloves, in Dai Bread's bakery flying like black flour, tonight in Donkey Street trotting silent, neddying among the snuggeries of babies, be dumbly royally winding through the Coronation cherry trees, going through the graveyard of Bethseda with winds gloved and folded, and dew doffed, tumbling by sailors' Arms, be slow, deep salt, and silent black, bandaged night . . .

In one line Chaucer writes:

> Night with his mantel, that is derk and rude
> Gan overspreyd . . .

and an ominousness settles over January's bridal bed. Dylan Thomas's "vitality" is really an abrogation of control over language, so that communication breaks down in a scattered plethora of random expressions as merely extravagant as a child's random babble. There is, as in the poetry, no controlling purpose to explore human reality. Of course, Thomas's audience listened, listening for the occasional salacious double meaning: the girls are "dreaming of the organ-playing wood," "The boys are dreaming wicked or of the bucking ranches of the night and the jollyrodgered sea." It is not quite obscene, but it sounds obscene, and it is for that school-boyish naughty talk that much of *Under Milk Wood* is endured by people who would never give half an ear to true dramatic poetry. It is a permitted "daftness" that by being a light relief from the dead dullness of everyday language in suburban England, leaves undisturbed this very deadness itself.

While the "poetic" parts of the writing draw attention to themselves self-consciously, the mood even becomes portentous as it echoes *East Coker*:

> *Time passes, Listen. Time passes.*
> *Come closer now.*

(cf. "If you do not come too close, if you do not come too close/ On a summer midnight . . .") But meanwhile, hypnotized by the patter and the *hwyl*, the listener or reader misses the implications of some of the more obsessional writing that recoils from reality as does some of the poetry:

> where the fish come biting out and nibble him down to his wishbone, and the long drowned muzzle up to him. He souses with the drowned and blowzy-breasted dead . . . Rosie Probert speaks from the bedroom of her dust . . .

We only fail to notice these disturbed notes because Thomas by his daft effervescence has reduced our response to language, destroyed an essential validity. If we are responding to poetry and drama our senses should be sharpened: in fact Thomas has an obsessive preoccupation with necrophiliac things, and mixes his obsession with corpses always with strong sexual overtones: here Captain Cat is obviously being nibbled in the genitals while sea-rotted corpses "nuzzle" up to him affectionately: he is breast to breast with corpses who are "blowsy-breasted"—presumably softly rotten, so that their breasts are soft like a woman's. Rosie Probert's "dust" is also her "bedroom": the intrusion on our senses is that of sexual intercourse with a corpse.

> Knock twice, Jack,
> at the door of my grave
> and ask for Rosie,

This morbid obsession of a necrophilic kind is a sick element in Thomas's writing and marks a flight from reality in which he seeks to involve us. The reader will protest that I am taking it too seriously: yet on the very next page to the line I quote above, Thomas attempts to write his most serious lines in this play:

Remember her.
She is forgetting,
The earth which filled her mouth
Is vanishing from her.
Remember me.
I have forgotten you.
I am going into the darkness of the darkness for ever.
I have forgotten that ever I was born.

The relationship between Captain Cat and Rosie Probert, whom he shared with Tom, Fred the Donkeyman and many other seaman is obviously important to Dylan Thomas, a point at which he is to invite our sympathy. Our sympathy is to be sharply drawn to the necrophilia itself—distasteful as it is—for Thomas is trying to involve us in his schizoid flight from reality. Captain Cat, having cried "Let me shipwreck in your thighs," is seen weeping. This is the *moment suprême* of the poetic drama.

But the lines quoted above reveal how short Thomas falls of anything approaching real drama of the *dromenon* or "thing done." The boyish view of the world, idiotically comic in places, has the interest of the boy's cruelty about adult human beings, and the excitement of naughty things seen and hinted at. But the test is the delineation of adult suffering: and here, where he attempts it, Dylan Thomas writes "Poetically" in another mode—the hortative empty mode of J. B. Priestley's pathetic attempt at poetic drama: *Johnson Over Jordan*:

> *Farewell all good things!*
> *You will not remember me,*
> *But I will remember you, . . .*

—an empty gesture far below the level of significance. What do Rosie's lines mean, beyond a gesture at feelings appropriate to dead people? If she is dead, how can she be "forgetting"? This is a dream of her, of course: but the lines take on a serious modulation (the rhythm having gone significantly flat) and we expect a general statement about Death. "The earth which filled her mouth / Is vanishing from her." What can this mean? "Getting a mouthful of mould" is a country expression, dry, ironic, stoical, for dying. But how "vanishing from her?" There is something about "vanishings from us" in a Georgian poem echoing Wordsworth's "fallings from us, vanishings"—and this kind of phrase seems distantly appropriate, as appropriate as robins are to Christmas. The origin of "I am going into the darkness of the darkness for ever" is plain enough: "They all go into the dark . . ." from Eliot's *Difficulties of a Statesman*.

But to return to Captain Cat and the nibbling fishes, there is an appropriate place in *Ulysses* at which we may usefully compare the playful immaturity of Thomas with the organized vitality of Joyce's best writing:

Five fathoms out there. Full fathom five thy father lies. At one he said. Found drowned, High water at Dublin Bar. Driving before it a loose drift of rubble, fanshoals of fishes, silly shells. A corpse rising white from the undertow, bobbing landward, a pace a pace a porpoise. There he is. Hook it quick. Sunk though he be beneath the watery floor. We have him. Easy now.

Bag of corpsegas sopping in foul brine. A quiver of minnows, fat of a spongy titbit, flash through the slits of his buttoned trouser fly. God becomes man becomes fish becomes barnacle goose becomes featherbed mountain.

Here is English prose whose effect is to satisfy us, even with a kind of elation. It may be an elation savoured with briny decay, but the writing moves, controlled, towards a philosophic contemplation of the tragic nature of life. It gains its intensity of realization—of appearances, movement, weight, texture, apprehension, rendered mental mood, from its moral intent, its moral, compassionate, consideration of man.

The rendering of the stream of Stephen Dedalus' consciousness demands a different kind of acceptance from the way we take the whimsy of Thomas's "wishbone" and "nuzzle." The concrete imagery ("fanshoals of fishes") and the movement ("We have him. Easy now") come as they flash on Stephen's inward eye in a particular mood. Not only are they realized by the movement of the prose, the corpse loosened in the flood tide, bobbing, and being grappled into a boat; but by these images the mood is realized in us. And the recollections of Shakespeare and other poets arise in complex with the imagery. Stephen's recoil from the sea, which he connects with his mother, her death, and his related sexual fears, is given us in the horrifying image of minnows fattening on a corpse's genitals, while this develops into a philosophical meditation (Stephen has not given up his faith without mental torment) and his knowledge of Elizabethan melancholy through Shakespeare ("a king may pass through the guts of a beggar"). The sequence ends in a fairy tale vision of a feather bed mountain, of vast indifferent insignificance, such as the human mind strives to come to terms with. Joyce's paragraphs have a wonderful economy, and the technique by which this is achieved was possible only by a profound morality: Stephen's agony of endeavouring to come to terms with life and death in a situation of disbelief and disintegrating values, to which his literary and philosophical training give him only fragmentary aid, is subtly given us. In experiencing it, we are experiencing the moral struggle of the contemporary consciousness. The struggle is given in such a verbal trick even as that "Pace a pace a porpoise," where, between "purpose" and "porpoise" we have the floating body as a symbol of both vitality and the end of life which "moves in this petty pace from day to day," as well as the pun on "sinkapace" and "cinquepace" (the dance) from Shakespeare.[1]

A great deal in *Under Milk Wood*, of course, derives directly from *Ulysses*: the names are an echo of Joyce's ironic use of them in the brothel scene. "Sinbad Sailors" is from "Sinbad the Sailor and Tinbad the Tailor" etc., and the rest are like a selection from Joyce's: Nogood Boyo equals Blazes Boylan, Mrs. Ogmore-Pritchard equals the Honourable Mrs. Mervyn Talboys, Rosie Probert equals either of the three whores of Bella Cohen or a character from Buck Mulligan's play, the Rev. Eli Jenkins equals the Reverend Mr. Haines Love or Father Malachi O'Flynn. Not that the characters are parallel, but the manner of naming representative types reflects Joyce's brothel scene. We have the children's rhymes and songs added, the "voices" giving elaborate "stage directions" like those in *Ulysses*, and so on.

These borrowings would not in themselves constitute a reprehensible plagiarism, for such contemporary works as *Ulysses* and *The Waste Land*, in developing new structures for the exploration of the contemporary consciousness, suggest new departures: and the brothel scene in *Ulysses* does suggest a mode of writing which can be more inclusive than the limits of conventional technique. But the use of the mode by borrowing the technique is a different matter from drawing cheques on the original work: Dylan Thomas's vitality, such as it is, is far too largely drawn from Joyce's own.

Take this passage, for instance:

FIRST VOICE   From where you are you can hear in Cockle Row in the Spring, moonless night, Miss Price, dressmaker and sweetshop-keeper, dream of

SECOND VOICE   her lover, tall as the town clock tower, Samson-syrup-gold-maned, whacking thighed and piping hot, thunderbolt bass'd and barnacle breasted, flailing up the cockles with his eyes like blow-lamps and scooping low over lonely loving hot-waterbottled body.

MR. EDWARDS   Myfanwy Price!

MISS PRICE   Mr. Mog Edwards!

MR. EDWARDS   I am a draper mad with love. I love you more than all the flannelette and calico, candle-wick, dimity, crush and merino, tussore, cretonne, crepon, muslin, poplin, ticking and twill in the whole Cloth Hall of the world. I have come to take you away to my Emporium on the hill, where the change hums on wires. Throw away your little bedsocks and your Welsh wool knitted jacket. I will warm the sheets like an electric toaster, I will lie by your side like the Sunday roast.

MISS PRICE   I will knit you a wallet of forget-me-not-blue, for the money to be comfy. I will warm your heart by the fire so that you can slip it under your vest when the shop is closed.

MR. EDWARDS   Myfanwy, Myfanwy, before the mice
gnaw at your Bottom drawer will you say

MISS PRICE   Yes, Mog, yes, Mog, yes, yes, yes,

MR. EDWARDS   And all the bells of the hills of the
town shall ring for our wedding.
[*Noise of money tills and chapel bells.*]

One could examine several other such passages to
discover what originality they contain of their own,
and what is borrowed. "Yes, Mog, yes, Mog, yes, yes,
yes," is from the end of *Ulysses:* "Yes and his heart
was going like mad and yes I said yes I will yes."
"Syrup-gold-maned" and "whacking thighed" are from
the Sirens episode in *Ulysses* ("Bronze by gold, Miss
Douce's head . . . sauntering gold hair . . . She
bronze, dealing from her jar thick syrup liquor for his
lips . . . and syrupped with her voice . . . neatly
she poured slowsyrupy sloe [2] . . . Smack. She let free
sudden in rebound her nipped elastic garter smack-
warm against her smackable woman's warmhosed
thigh . . ."). While Mr. Bloom eats, Pollard "bas-
sooned attack, booming over bombarding chords"
"base barreltone." The suggestiveness of "flailing up
the cockles" (with his eyes? How?) is reminiscent of
Joyce's "with a cock with a carra" and the name "Paul
de Kock": Joyce's has more than a suggestive double
meaning because the note sounded by "cock-crow" in
the siren scene is for Bloom one of betrayal. Blazes
Boylan is the cock crowing over him and the Petrine
cock is to change into a cuckoo, because he is cuckold:
in Thomas the meaningless phrase seems to be there
merely for suggestiveness' sake. "Lonely" springs too
from "I feel so lonely, Bloom," a reminiscence with
point from the correspondence between "Henry
Flower" and Martha the typist, at a point when
Bloom writes his "Henry Flower" letter, while Blazes

Boylan is drinking preparatory to ravishing Mrs. Bloom. The rest of the quotation is also reminiscent of the section of *Ulysses* where Mr. Bloom gets into bed with his wife, the rhythm of "her lonely loving hot-waterbottled body" reminiscent of "the plump mellow yellow melons of her rump," etc. The "inspiration" behind the love-dream in *Under Milk Wood* is all too patently derived from *Ulysses:* to portray his comic lovers, Thomas draws not on actual, but literary experience, and that he does so contributes to the quality I have described as "areal." He makes Joyce's controlled Rabelaisian bawdy into mere urchin daftness.

Dylan Thomas's deficiency of moral interest in his characters manifests itself in the lack of economy and order in his use of his material. Set against a representative passage of Joyce his collections of images appear unrelated and unco-ordinated. Mr. Mog Edwards may be compared, in terms of the moral interest of a character, with James Houghton in Lawrence's *The Lost Girl.* There Lawrence's catalogues of stuffs, which Dylan Thomas's list in the passage just quoted recalls, show both that Lawrence knew the stuffs vividly at first hand, far more so than Thomas, and also that he uses them both as a comment on his draper, his attitude to Woodhouse, and the nature of Woodhouse itself:

> They wearied James Houghton with their demand for common zephyrs, for red flannel which they would scallop with black worsted, for black alpacas and bombazines and merinos. He fluffed out his silk-striped muslins, his India cotton prints. But the natives shied off as if he had offered them the poisoned robes of Herakles.

The movement and sound of that are the assurance of a writer who knows what he is doing, has "placed" his characters morally. And so the humour ("common zephyrs" "the poisoned robes of Herakles") has a keen edge in the texture of the writing.

Similarly James Joyce's bizarrest visions have a moral faculty, sustained by the control of language:

THE HONOURABLE MRS. MERVYN TALBOYS
(In amazon costume, hard hat, jack boots cockspurred vermillion waistcoat, fawn musketeer gauntlets with braided drums, long train held up and hunting crop with which she strikes her welt constantly.)

Here the choice of words convinces us that the things are seen and felt ("with braided drums"): Mrs. Talboys is accurately costumed in the articles of wear for which Bloom has a perverted relish. The vision tells us much about Bloom's imagination: he is abasing himself in horror of his "crimes" but enjoying both the recollection and the abasement and guilt ("*He pants cringing*," "*I love the danger*"). The neatness and vitality of language ("cockspurred," and the suggestive force of "welt") maintain a healthiness of ironic *timbre* and wit in the midst of the realization of unpleasant masochism and perverted impotence. And, ironically, again, the Mrs. Talboys of Bloom's vision goes on to speak in a high moral tone ("This plebian Don Juan . . . urged me . . . to sin") but by certain lapses ("he sent me an obscene photograph . . . insulting to any lady. *I have it still*") betrays a morality parallel to Bloom's, and thus the passage is high comedy of a moral order—Jonsonian. The implications are similar to those of Lear's speech about the Beadle whipping the whore who "hotly lusts to use her in that kind for which thou whipst her": "None does offend, none": the theme is the general collapse of morality. Only Joyce's vitality of language preserves a positive ground to explore his horrors. Because he has no such moral capacity Dylan Thomas's vitality becomes haphazard, breathless and overdone, its interest merely verbal.

Dylan Thomas's lack of moral control has been called (by Mr. Vernon Watkins) "a rooted opposition to material progress": but it would seem very different from D. H. Lawrence's "rooted opposition" to the drives of our society, which never lost the tenderness of knowing poignantly, as with Gerald Crich in *Women in Love*, the individual human consequences of mechanical civilization which *all* suffer in the same degree. We miss in *Under Milk Wood* as in Thomas's poetry the essential compassion of the true artist.

In Dylan Thomas the vibration against suburbia is commingled with a tone of revolt which seems to spring from a lack of assurance that he was as superior to the suburbians as he makes himself out to be. "The jerry villa'd and smug-suburbed snug, smug, trim, middling prosperous suburb of my utterly confining outer world . . ."—the suburban world is rejected because it confined him, not because it imprisons other human beings: the vibration of the sentence shows the writer's uncertainty as to whether he has ever really escaped. The same degree of vibration is absent from Lawrence's calmer tone:

> And at the same instant, came the ironical question 'What for?' She thought of the colliers' wives, with their linoleum and their lace curtains and their little girls in high-laced boots. She thought of the wives and daughters of the pit-managers, their tennis parties, and their terrible struggles to be superior to each other in the social scale . . .

Lawrence *places* people as beings, in such a way as to escape himself from snobbery, and the sense of superiority to them: he has no need to feel uncertain about his own status—he has escaped, he is his own nature's rare creature. Dylan Thomas exerts only a personal antipathy against people leading ordinary lives, in decency and good relationship, because they threaten him with reality. Throughout his work there is a recurrent cruel animus—that of the emotionally insecure infant: "Take old Bennet and whip him down the corridor . . . hammer his teeth back into his prim, bald, boring head" (*Adventures in the Skin Trade*, p. 23). And after locking the train lavatory door on someone: " 'I bet you're dancing,' he said to the other person the other side of the locked door" (p. 33). Such cruelty is of infantile oral sadism.

"We're all mad and nasty," says Mr. Allingham in the same book, and this often seems the writer's attitude to people. Dylan Thomas's "revolt" against suburbia consists largely in exhibiting "sin" as amusing for its own sake: in *Adventures in the Skin Trade*, when a character enters saying he has just drunk forty-nine Guinnesses, we are expected to laugh simply at that. We may compare Falstaff's "A pox on this gout or a gout on this pox . . ." which is evocative of a sensuality which in its bravado against the weak body and death is a kind of courage, however misplaced. But Shakespeare places Falstaff as one who does not accept mortality, and is therefore both unable to deal with life and outstandingly subject to mortality: he is told, "Fall to thy prayers." Dylan Thomas (whose vision, according to Mr. Watkins, again, is "essentially tragic") on "The Death of Comic Writers" said: "Society to a comic writer is always funny, even, or especially, on its death bed . . . a writer creating a great comic world out of the tragic catastrophe of this" (*Quite Early One Morning*, p. 122). But Thomas, though he took himself seriously with the "noble" earnestness of a child, lacks the needful gravity and sense of reality to write tragedy. "Sin" is fascinating, and sin is dirty postcards, booze, winking at women, peeping through keyholes and locking people out of lavatories. Through the appeal of these we become involved in the impulses of the child-spirit who desires savagely to deny his own need to accept growth, time, love and death:

> Cheater at patience, keyhole peeper, keeper of nail-clippings and ear-wax; lusting after silhouettes on Laburnam's blind, searching for thighs in the library of classical favourites, Sam Thumb in the manhole prying up on windy days . . . (*Adventures in the Skin Trade*, p. 45.)

To the true artist, like Joyce, petty sins in themselves are unimportant, and are presented against a larger background which makes them poignantly trivial and deserving of our deepest compassion because they manifest a larger failure. Take, for instance, Joyce's portrayal of Bloom as a *voyeur*. Such weaknesses are indices to Joyce of deeper sorrows and moral weaknesses, in our civilization. English suburbia, while it hides its psychic woes under a surface respectability, gossips and guffaws with Dylan Thomas over the petty sins which it outwardly conceals under prurient taboos. Dylan Thomas reinforces a respectability which can only maintain its pretences by denying so much in life.

This piece is at its best when engaged in caricature removed from reality—as with Mrs. Ogmore-Pritchard, for instance. It is at its worst when it approaches real human life and emotion—for example, when Polly Garter speaks to her baby, in the delineation of the Cherry Owens, and in the serious passages between Captain Cat and Rosie Probert. At times the author employs, as with Mrs. Willy Nilly, a simple and misapplied Freudianism ("every night of her life she had been late for school")—hinting, with a naughty leer, that you will find, under the surface, people's impulses governed by their childhood sins, you will find in their inward selves dirty dreams and wicked desires. But this use of "Freudian" psychology is, of course, here employed to plead for Thomas's own immature impulses themselves.

In *Under Milk Wood* there is not one positive love relationship—only with Rosie Probert (dead) and Polly Garter (indifferent). How is it that Dylan Thomas can offer us Llaregyb as "a place of love"? Significantly the phrase is associated with the word "dust"—and we remember "his mother's breast, which was rest—and dust":

> Each cobble, donkey, goose and gooseberry street is a thoroughfare of dust; and dusk and ceremonial dust, and night's first darkening snow, and the sleep of birds, drift under and through the live dust of this place of love. Llaregyb is the capital of dusk.

This expression is typically approached through the establishment, hypnotically, of elevation of mood, by the anaesthetic *hwyl*. A special plea is being made for Llaregyb as the place of the child-love—the seaside of Thomas's childhood where he walked with his mother in Paradise, and where he attempts to lead his child-like adulthood. The passage is followed immediately by the culmination of the child's hostile rendering of married love—as with Mr. Pugh with a "poker backed nutcracker wife"—in Mrs. Ogmore-Pritchard and her two hag-ridden husbands.

Before we examine Mrs. Ogmore-Pritchard, let us first take a perspective of Llaregyb as "a place of love." The place of childish love—as in the poems—takes two forms. One relates to the child's

> *Forgotten mornings when he walked with his mother*
> *Through the parables*
> *Of sun light*
> *And the legends of the green chapels* . . .

where "One sun, one manna, warmed and fed"—the mother's all satisfying breast. And this goes with the breathless, incoherent child-babble, to create an illusory reality that transcends the actual reality: "It is spring, moonless night in the small town, starless/and bible-black . . ." And as I have tried to show in discussing the poems, this illusory world, in which everything gyrates round the noble child-figure, could not protect Thomas from the pressure of reality. The pressure comes from the demands made on an adult to love, and allow himself to be loved. In a number of poignant poems he reveals himself to be unable to yield in love, because it seems to him like a death; the growth to personal mature reality and fulfilment in time is deathly:

> Time held me green and dying,
> Though I sang in my chains like the sea.

The clues to the sexual failure are in *I make this in a warring absence, Not From this Anger,* and *Holy Spring,* in which the "immortal hospital of love" has made "one more move to soothe/The cureless counted body."

The sexual failure—the failure, that is, to accept love between a man and a woman—escapes into playful necrophilia. And in *Under Milk Wood* this dead-love becomes the relationship between Captain Cat and his dead loved ones, including Rosie Probert. The failure is, too, represented as a belief that the tenderest sex is that of the whore—Polly Garter's memory of Little Willie Wee—who, of course, is the child-Thomas himself who, as a child, had potency (see *In the White Giant's Thigh*). But, again, characteristically, and necrophiliac-wise, "little Willy Wee is dead, dead, dead." And Polly thinks of him whenever she jumps into the arms of another "good bad boy from the lonely farms." She is at the end copulating with Mr. Waldo—I use the term advisedly, because the man is drunk, and the act is coldly sensual, though Thomas is not able to render it to us as such, placed:

> And Mr. Waldo drunk in the dusky wood hugs his lovely Polly Garter under the eyes and rattling tongues of the neighbours and the birds, and he does not care.
> He smacks his live red lips.
> But it is not *his* name that Polly Garter whispers as she lies under the oak and loves him back. Six feet deep that name sings in the cold earth.

POLLY GARTER [*sings*] But I always think as we tumble into bed . . .

We may note that "he licks his live red lips": the powerful special plea is being made for our tolerance of desperate and ugly sensuality. We take it as meaning "live and let live": it is powerfully shot through with the implication that "to be alive is to behave like this." Note the special pleading in *"She loves him back"*: in the circumstances, he drunk, she dreaming of Willy Wee—would she be likely to?

By cunning means Thomas seeks to weave us into a mood of tolerance of reality-denial: opposition to sexual promiscuity is meanwhile caricatured in Jack Black. The potentialities of life-long love in marriage are caricatured in Mrs. Ogmore-Pritchard, in the two Mrs. Dai Breads, in Mr. and Mrs. Pugh. Only the Cherry Owens are sympathetically portrayed—and we shall see soon that there is another cunning special plea woven into them—the plea for the "little weakness" of the alcoholic. The whole picture of this "place of love" is essentially one which denies the reality of love and the possibility of adequate adult relationship.

The attitude to sexual love in *Under Milk Wood* is

that of the late poem *Lament*. The childish anarchy of this poem may be compared with the stern, if pitying, recognition in folk-song of the ravages of time, and the pitfalls of love, and of sexual reality. (Compare *A Young Sailor Cut Down in His Prime*, for instance.) *Lament* is no account of the sexual reality—it is a special plea for the kind of self-destructive denial of reality to which Thomas himself, the child who is unable to grow up, had come.

In *If my Head hurt a Hair's foot* and *Vision and Prayer* for instance we have delineated the strange resentment in Thomas at new birth as the outcome of sexual union. But we do not see these implications because we are disarmed, by the child-appeal. The wide appeal of *Under Milk Wood* is, of course, in its childish dirty jokes. Wit at the level of the radio programme is combined with the innuendo of the commercial traveller's and the schoolboy's sex-anxious tale. Suburbia is happy to find such boosts to its respectability in "highbrow" "art."

> *it's organ organ all the time with him . . .*
> *Parley-vous jig-jig, Madam?*
> *I'll never have such*
> *ding a ding*
> *again . . .*
> *everytime she shakes its slap slap slap . . .*
> *P. C. Attila Rees has got his truncheon out . . .*
> *the bushy tail wags rude and ginger . . .*
> *Give him sennapods and lock him in the dark . . .*
> *I will lie by your side like the Sunday roast*
> *before the mice gnaw at your bottom drawer . . .*
> *all cucumber and hooves . . .*

Some of this is not better or worse than music-hall smut and patter: but in a work which sets out to be serious it needs to be controlled, as Ben Jonson's bawdy is, by a deep ironic perception. Here it is merely obscene suggestiveness:

Gossamer Benyon high-heels out of school. The sun hums down through the cotton flowers of her dress into the bell of her heart and bees in the honey there and couches and kisses, lazy-loving and boozed, in her red-berried breast . . .

Eyes run from the trees and windows of the street, steaming 'Gossamer' and strip her to the nipples and the bees . . . Sinbad Sailor places on her thighs still dew-damp from the first mangrowing cock-crow garden his reverent goat-bearded hands . . .

GOSSAMER BENYON   So long as he's all cucumber and hooves

SECOND VOICE   She feels his goatbeard tickle her in the middle of the world like a tuft of wiry fire . . .

The excitement of Thomas's suggestive passages depends upon the presence of recoil and shame; here "hums," for instance, has a flavour of distaste in the attitude towards: "lazy-loving and boozed in her red-berried breast" reveals an excitement which comes not from outward-turning sympathy and placing of a character, but an urge to self-stimulus: we feel all too embarrassingly the presence of the author's needs. The reader may compare Dylan Thomas's line on his penis "my cherry-capped dangler" in *Once Below a Time* with D. H. Lawrence's poem *Virgin Youth* and Robert Graves's *Down! Wanton, Down!* as differences between prudishness and honesty: and between auto-eroticism and compassionate maturity in sexual explicitness. So "strip her to the nipples," "mangrowing cock-crow," "goatbearded," "cucumber" and so forth have the same auto-erotic mental stimulus here as words in dirty jokes have for the schoolboy—this prose is offered with no controlling irony: yet this is Dylan Thomas's "vitality." (We may remember how Joyce "places" Mrs. Bloom, by making her, in the shame of her adultery, want to shout out obscene words.)

To assist the disarming of the audience, morality is pilloried by the rendering of the castigator of sin, who himself commits the worse sin of enjoying sin:

Jack Black prepares once more to meet his Satan in the wood. He grinds his teeth, closes his eyes, climbs into his religious trousers, their flies sewn up with cobbler's thread, and pads out, torched and bibled, grimly, joyfully, into the already sinning dusk.

But even he, it will be noted, is presented in the same manner and rhythm, without attitude towards of disapproval or sympathy, only as for every character, of derision. Everyone among the characters is a *lovable* derision-deserving caricature; there is no good, no bad, no complexity, no change—and so no life. No beastliness is met with anything but laughter, and "the boys will be boys" attitude obviously so dear to the writer's flight from the demands of adult life. With the Cherry Owens he indicates twice in stage directions, strangely, that they should "laugh with delight." The repetition of this exhortation shows how uncertain the writer was that this hopelessly unconvincing exchange (under the circumstances) would be acceptable to the reader:

MRS. CHERRY OWEN   See that smudge on the wall by the picture of Auntie Blossom?
That's where you threw the sago
[*Cherry Owen laughs with delight*]
Remember last night? In you reeled, my boy, as drunk as a deacon, with a big wet bucket and a fish-pail full of stout, and you looked at me and said "God has come home". . .
And then you took off your trousers and you said 'Does anybody want a fight?'
Oh, you old baboon . . .
Then you danced on the table all over again and said you were King Solomon Owen and I was your Mrs. Sheba.

CHERRY OWEN [softly] And then?

MRS. CHERRY OWEN And then I got you into bed
and you snored all night like a brewery.

[Mr. and Mrs. Cherry Owen laugh delightedly to-
gether].

How delightful! A world in which all women would
mother their men, and laugh delightedly at drunken-
ness! How delightful if love-making fails in the impotence of alcoholic sleep, and desire always outlives
performance—and the women never complain, but
laugh, delightedly! What a delightful world! A world
in which there is no reality and decent human feelings
do not exist! The episode should be read in the light of
Karl Menninger's comments quoted above (Introduction p. 14): it is the alcoholic's wish to "overlook
. . . serious aggression."

In *Under Milk Wood* the children, like the Child-
Thomas, are less a glimpse of innocence than symbols
of a yearning for the undiscriminating and unreal
attitude to experience for which Thomas himself has a
damaging nostalgia:

> gobstoppers big as wens that rainbow as you suck,
> brandyballs, winegums, hundreds and thousands, liquo-
> rice sweet as sick, nougat to tug and ribbon out like
> another red rubbery tongue, gum to glue in girl's curls,
> crimson coughdrops to spit blood, ice-cream cornets,
> dandelion and burdock, raspberry and cherryade, pop
> goes the weasel and the wind . . .

I find the role of the children in *Under Milk Wood*
and their "traditional" songs not very profound or
convincing. Thomas is in fact not really interested in
children—other children—but only in himself as child.
The conversation of Polly Garter with her baby is
again a plea for an impossible infantile moral anarchy—there is no suffering here, even though the
child does not know which is its father, of Polly's many

casual sexual partners: "Me, Polly Garter, under the washing line, giving the breast in the garden to my bonny new baby . . ." (Note the force of that "bonny"—it has the same false ring as the "delight-edly" in Thomas's account of the Cherry Owens in denying reality.)

> Nothing grows in our garden, only washing. And babies. And where's their fathers live, my love? Over the hills and far away. You're looking up at me now. I know what you're thinking, you poor little milky creature. You're thinking, you're no better than you should be, Polly, and that's good enough for me. Oh, isn't life a terrible thing, thank God?
>
> [*Single long high chord on strings*]

The stage direction for music emphasizes the urgency of Thomas's desire to convince us that in this unreal world there is no suffering, as a consequence of the kind of "love" he himself is forced by his sickness to seek—that is, the satisfaction of sexual needs without the acceptance of responsibility. For a moment, in his need for maternal solace, he is lying himself on Polly Garter's breast: Polly expresses the sentiments that excuse him—"that's good enough for me": "Oh isn't life a terrible thing, thank God?" "we're all mad and nasty"—"life is terrible." But the predominate urge is to be treated like a child. The unreality lies in the utter impossibility of such a complacent speech, in any real sense, from such a woman who in actual life would suffer in many ways from her weaknesses, and deserve our pity, as would her children.

Thomas sets out to expose the hatred of life he sup-poses in the clean neat suburban home: in this sense he may be said to have struck out a little "for life"—but the deathly hygienic denial of Mrs. Ogmore-Pritchard is but the obverse of his own shrinking from the actualities of bodily sex, his recoil from giving himself in love to another being, his sensational obsession with death. He hates and fears life as much as this himself.

Now, in her ice-berg-white, holily laundered crinoline nightgown, under virtuous polar sheets, in her spruced and scoured dust-defying bedroom in trig and trim Bay View, a house for paying guests, at the top of the town, Mrs. Ogmore-Pritchard widow, twice, of Mr. Ogmore, linoleum, retired, and Mr. Pritchard, failed bookmaker, who, maddened by besoming, swabbing and scrubbing, the voice of the vacuum cleaner and the fume of polish, ironically swallowed disinfectant, fidgets in her rinsed sleep, wakes in a dream, and nudges in the ribs dead Mr. Ogmore, dead Mr. Pritchard, ghostly on either side.

MRS. OGMORE-PRITCHARD   Mr. Ogmore!
Mr. Pritchard!
It is time to inhale your balsam.

MR. OGMORE   Oh, Mrs. Ogmore!

MR. PRITCHARD   Oh, Mrs. Pritchard!

MRS. PRITCHARD   Soon it will be time to get up.
Tell me your tasks in order.

MR. OGMORE   I must put my pyjamas in the drawer marked pyjamas.

MR. PRITCHARD   I must take my cold bath which is good for me . . .

MR. OGMORE   I must blow my nose.

MRS. OGMORE-PRITCHARD   In the garden if you please.

MR. OGMORE   In a piece of tissue paper which I afterwards burn . . .

MR. PRITCHARD   I must dust the blinds and then I must raise them.

MRS. OGMORE-PRITCHARD   And before you let the sun in, mind it wipes its shoes.

But the episode slops over into morbid sensationalism, even so:

FIRST VOICE   And in through the keyhole, *with tears where their eyes once were*, they ooze and grumble . . .

MRS. OGMORE-PRITCHARD   Husbands . . . I love you both.

MR. OGMORE [*with terror*]   Oh, Mrs. Ogmore.

MR. PRITCHARD [*with horror*]   Oh, Mrs. Pritchard.
                                   [Italics supplied]

And typically ends in a hideous vision of Mrs. Ogmore-Pritchard in sexual union with her ghosts, an unfortunate and childish lapse into a different plane, the necrophiliac jest turning away any expectation of a genuine "criticism of life" and revealing only Thomas's own hatred.

> Soon it will be time to go bed. Tell me your tasks in order.

MR. OGMORE AND MR. PRITCHARD   We must take our pyjamas from the drawer marked pyjamas.

MRS. OGMORE-PRITCHARD [*Coldly*]   And then you must take them off.

One successful comic theme and some hilarity does not, I suggest, make a poetic drama of the kind of significance claimed for this work. There is a lively delineation of characters and their background, sometimes with a gesture at a "Freudian" explanation of their behaviour as with Mrs. Willy Nilly, and a little vitality of observation of human nature. But there could not be any moral development, because throughout the whole of his work Dylan Thomas is concerned with only one thing: to vindicate his own schizoid inability to accept as an adult the reality of human existence. To have accepted the full human reality of any character, or the real interaction of characters, to have escaped from his areal toy-village, to have exposed his own special pleas for sensual indulgence would have been too painful. To have begun to enact moral choice, embodied aspects of human experience in conflict, good against evil, love against lust, maturity against immaturity, reality against appearances and self-deceptions, this would have required a vast enlargement of the true voice, the true self-knowledge such as Thomas displays in his few true poems—*Out of the Sighs, I have longed to move away, Should lanterns shine, O make me a mask*. But Llaregyb itself was spun out of the false gabble of Llareggub, the world of half-art, and language with no vital engagement on life, with the help of the half-educated audience of English suburbia. It remains a plea for a schizoid detachment from reality, in Thomas, and in the culture in which he became so popular. That Llaregyb can be accepted by us as "a place of love," in all its ugliness and half-humanity is a disturbing feature of our cultural predicament. That the Llareggubian language, concealing the true voice, the language of the "mask" of self-deception is so widely acclaimed reveals a debility in our higher literacy. There is in *Under Milk Wood* no bad and no good—there is no moral discrimination which can help us to live. It may, of course, command our pity and dismay that Dylan Thomas spent his whole life disguising his weaknesses and endeavouring to involve his readers in them, to the lessening, if anything, of their powers of living. His own attitude to experience is too much that of such a character as his Mae Rose Cottage who draws lipstick circles round her nipples (the image is there to involve us in "naughty" delight) and cries,

> *I'm fast. I'm a bad lot, God will strike me dead.*
> *I'm seventeen. I'll go to hell . . . you just wait.*
> *I'll sin till I blow up.*

Our reactions to the "naughtiness" in Dylan Thomas's work tend to involve us in feelings which are governed by our wanting to make allowances for this writer, as if for a child: symptomatically, he was called everywhere by his Christian name. What are the implications, about our society, our literary minority, when such a writer is so popular, a writer who essentially provokes a nostalgia for an irresponsible but noble childhood in which adult dealings with reality are avoided and denied? Such art can hardly help us in our dealing with life. Art would seem to me, if it is worth our allegiance in terms of effort and respect, to be justified by the deep satisfactions it may give in terms of advanced maturity, of developed personal integration and a more developed reality sense—bringing greater insight and understanding. This is not Dylan Thomas's contribution.

NOTES

1 — Introduction

1. D. W. Winnicott, *Collected Papers* (London: Tavistock Press, 1958).

2. These paragraphs are a bald and over-simple statement of problems of the formation of consciousness based on theories of such recent psychoanalytical writers as Melanie Klein and D. W. Winnicott in England. A more full account will appear in the present writer's *The Quest for Love* (London: Methuen, 1964). An earlier "classic" essay is "The problem of Acceptance of Unpleasant Ideas" by Sandor Ferenczi, in *Further Contributions to the Theory and Technique of Psycho-Analysis* (Institute of Psycho-Analysis, 1960).

3. In *The Origins of Love and Hate* (1935), a critique of Freudian psychology.

4. See E. P. Thompson, *The Making of the English Working Class* (London: Gollancz, 1963).

5. Cf. Dylan Thomas, "I found a bottle of foetus": *The Mouse and the Woman.* The image turned up again the other day in a poem about a glass paper weight by Sylvia Plath.

6. I do not mean the genital kiss is disgusting.

7. See R. D. Laing, *The Divided Self* (London: Tavistock Press, 1960).

8. Karl Menninger, *Man Against Himself* (New York: Harvest Books, 1938).

2 — The True Voice of English Poetry

1. Readers of *English for Maturity* will, I hope, pardon my use here of some material somewhat similar to material in that book in the discussion of metaphor.

3—Critical Self-Deception

1. *Hwyl* is the Welsh term for the ecstatic state into which an eloquent preacher works himself.

2. Mr. John Bayley in *The Romantic Survival* (p. 215) says of Dylan Thomas's poetry, apparently approvingly, "the sensation is that we are being assaulted by something other than words." This is true, but the assault is a verbal sensationalism energetically cloaking reality, and doing so for the same reasons of oral aggression as alcoholism. The effect is thus the reverse of that of metaphor. See p. 15 above.

4—Some of Them May Be Poems

1. Cf. Edith Sitwell in *The Atlantic*: "His reddish amber curls, strong as the curls on the brow of a young bull," etc.

2. Mrs. Nowottny says "armless love" means the Venus de Milo because this statue lacks arms. The same critic says that "murdering breath" recalls Swinburne's "the world has grown grey with thy breath." From this she deduces a vision of the German Army whose uniforms were grey; therefore Christ equals Hitler. But Thomas doesn't use the word "grey"! I can only find such dissociated ingenuity ludicrous—but it is an industry Thomas inevitably fosters, because he was so careless about meaning.

3. D. W. Winnicott in *Collected Papers* gives accounts of the dreams of patients in psychoanalysis which associate the "armless" movements of the foetus in the birth passage during parturition with the thrusting phallus. This is the root of some aberrations, and may be the unconscious origin of Thomas's choice of this odd word.

4. I suppose a cut throat might be said to have a mouth which was also a sexual object, as in Baudelaire's

> *Et faire à ton flanc étonné*
> *Une blessure large et creuse,*
>
> *Et, vertigineuse douceur!*
> *A travers ces lèvres nouvelles,*
> *Plus éclatantes et plus belles,*
> *T'infuser mon venin, ma soeur!*
>
> A CELLE QUI EST TROP GAI.

Thomas mimics unsuccessfully this kind of desperate sensuality, at second hand.

5—A Deadness of Rhythm

1. A useful comparison not unrelated to Dylan Thomas is to contrast the vitality of Marlowe's great line "See, see where Christ's blood streams in the firmament" and the rest of a poem by Edith Sitwell, *Still Falls the Rain*, in which she quotes it. Despite a structure owing something to Eliot's Ash Wednesday ("have mercy on us") her rhythms are those of Swinburne and nineteenth-century hymns.

2. Thomas's mistake has been to take over this from Hopkins's *Spelt from Sibyl's leaves*: "Only the beak-leaved boughs dragonish damask the tool-smooth bleak light; black . . ."

3. Cf. Daniel Jones in *Dylan Thomas, the Legend and the Poet*: "We had word obsessions: everything at one time was 'little' or 'white'; and sometimes an adjective became irresistibly funny in almost any connection: 'innumerable bananas', 'wilful moccasins', 'a certain Mrs. Prothero'. These word-games, and even the most facetious of our collaborations, had a serious experimental purpose, and there is no doubt that they played an important part in Dylan's early poetic development."

4. The line "Blaspheme down the stations of the breath" has a texturally unfortunate irrelevant suggestion of steam trains.

5. See the quotation from Suzanne Roussillat given in the first part of Chapter 7 below p. 137.

7—"A Place of Love": Under Milk Wood

1. "And sinkapace into his grave"—*Much Ado About Nothing*. Mr. Michael Black adds to my note: "A porpoise bobs up rhythmically. So, as the corpse breaks water rhythmically it reminds Stephen of the porpoise, and of a dance—and perhaps of the vitality of the sexual act. 'A pace a pace' also suggests the gentle progression in the tide."

2. Note above Dylan Thomas's pun on "sloe" and "slow."

INDEX